ENTREPRENEURIAL WOMEN WHO LIVE THE LIVES THEY WANT:

"I'm making more money than I ever made before, and it feels good. I like being my own boss and setting my own time schedule. I like the tax benefits and I like belonging to professional organizations. And I love the freedom!"
—Karen Sandler, interior plant landscaper

"As an actor, I complained about the poor roles available for women. Now I'm in a position to do something about it."
—Nancy Malone, independent film producer

"I get so much pleasure out of taking care of myself . . . I have the freedom to make my own decisions and set my own goals. I can explore my creativity. The only limits I have are my own."
—Sanda Alcalay, owner of French Conversational Seminars and Aubergine and Associates, Catered Affairs

THE ENTREPRENEURIAL WOMAN
"Covers everything from bankruptcy to riches . . . How to handle jealousy, competition . . . male chauvinism, sex discrimination, sexual advances, and the conflict of trying to be a homemaker and businesswoman at the same time."
—*Christian Science Monitor*

The Entrepreneurial Woman

by Sandra Winston

BANTAM BOOKS
Toronto / New York / London

THE ENTREPRENEURIAL WOMAN
*A Bantam Book/published by arrangement with
Newsweek Books*

PRINTING HISTORY
*Newsweek edition published March 1979
A Selection of Woman Today Book Club May 1979
Bantam edition/October 1980*

*All rights reserved.
Copyright © 1979 by Sandra Winston
Cover art copyright © 1980 by Bantam Books.
This book may not be reproduced in whole or in part, by
mimeograph or any other means, without permission.
For information address: Newsweek Books,
444 Madison Avenue,
New York, N.Y. 10022*

ISBN 0-553-13479-5

Published simultaneously in the United States and Canada

Bantam Books are published by Bantam Books, Inc. Its trademark, consisting of the words "Bantam Books" and the portrayal of a bantam, is Registered in U.S Patent and Trademark Office and in other countries Marca Registrada Bantam Books, Inc , 666 Fifth Avenue New York, New York 10103

PRINTED IN THE UNITED STATES OF AMERICA

0 9 8 7 6 5 4 3 2 1

For my husband, George,
and our children,
Marci, Gregg, and Robin.

Contents

Foreword 9

Introduction 11

1
Entrepreneurship ... is it for you? 21

2
Entrepreneurship ... do you have the resources? 45

3
What kind of business? 65

4
Self-confidence 85

5
Learning to be assertive 103

6
A woman's place is in the home ... or is it? 123

7
Stress and the entrepreneurial woman 145

8
Learning the hard way . . .
things your lawyer or accountant never told you 163

9
Starting your own business 181

10
That first sale . . . I didn't even know what to charge 199

11
Bankruptcy can be beautiful 213

12
Achievement and its rewards 223

Suggested Reading 236
Acknowledgements 239

Foreword

While many articles and books have been written on the "how to's" of starting your own business, this book is the first to focus on the psychological and personal implications for women.

The potential woman entrepreneur may be a teacher, nurse, secretary, or any woman stuck in a job that does not fulfill her or which does not bring sufficient income. The entrepreneurial woman is simply the woman who wants to start her own business.

Women in the business world have always been forced to juggle their lives between their work and their families or to choose between careers and marriage. They may run from a conference with Susie's teacher to a conference with their sales manager. These problems are faced by the woman with a nine-to-five job, but they have the greatest impact on the woman entrepreneur. No one can cover for her. She's caught by family responsibilities on the one hand and her responsibilities to her career on the other. The buck stops with her. No one pays for her vacations or sick leave.

By sharing the experiences, trials, and successes of other women in business, this book gives the needed support and encouragement to those women who are thinking of going it on their own in the business world. There is help for the new entrepreneurial woman, the reentry woman, the woman considering a career change, and the professional contemplating whether or not private practice is for her.

Introduction

It's lunchtime, Thursday, and this is crazy! Instead of opening a can of tuna in my kitchen, I'm prying open a huge lobster claw at New York's Palm Restaurant, thousands of miles from my kitchen. My husband, George, is with me. We're lunching with the vice-president of network TV programming from George's advertising agency, and I can't believe what he is discussing . . . a TV special built around my book. And he's serious! This has been a very exciting day—sessions with publishers, publicists, and promoters. And now, I'm talking about a TV show. THE ENTREPRENEURIAL WOMAN . . . THAT'S ME!! Lobster never tasted better.

I look at the lobster, the vice-president, the lobster, my husband, the lobster, and "CLICK" . . . LOBSTER! What a symbol for me! There it sits on the plate, shell split open, so delicious . . . and so vulnerable. Lobsters do all their growing after shedding their shells, when they're most vulnerable.

How many shells have I broken out of these past few years? What is this suburban housewife, mother of three, former speech therapist and teacher, doing here? How did it all begin? Where did I start?

I remember Gregg's little hand in mine as we crossed the street, but I knew things would be different next year. He'd go off to nursery school and I'd be alone. I'd seen it happen two years earlier when Marci started school and I wondered what I'd ever

Introduction

do to keep occupied with both children in school. The year was 1966. The place was Cincinnati, Ohio. The ideal American family consisted of a mother, three kids, a dog, a home in the suburbs, a station wagon, and a commuting dad. Our family had everything but the third kid and the station wagon. Since I never wanted to own a station wagon, the choice was easy. A few months later the deed was accomplished and I was pregnant. Robin was born in May of 1967. For the next two years, I enjoyed my role as stay-at-home mother again. But this time I felt more like a grandmother, playing with Robin, dressing her up, and taking her everywhere I went. It was so much fun, but so short-lived. Too soon it was time for her to start nursery school, and I knew I'd have to find something new to fill my life.

I'd had enough of being a speech therapist; and PTA, tennis, and volunteer work were beginning to pall. I felt a need to expand my mind, so I was off to graduate school. Since I couldn't get the tuition money by economizing on my food budget, nor from my husband (he thought grad school was just another of my "hobbies"), I applied for a graduate fellowship in Learning Disabilities (LD) and Special Education. It was a wide-open field. I was sure I could get the fellowship, since my speech therapy experience was related, and I did. September 1972 found me enrolled as a full-time graduate student at the University of Cincinnati. I'd asked George for permission to return to school, and he'd said, in effect, "OK... Do anything, just as long as the socks are folded, it doesn't cost me any money, the dinner's on the table, and it doesn't inconvenience me." Sounded like a fair deal, so I accepted. Well, it took me about three months to figure out that I'd made a bad deal. I was not Wonder Woman. Going to school daily from 2:30 until 7:00 PM with three young children and a hungry husband at home wasn't as easy as I'd imagined. But I knew one thing... I was going to get that degree!

Two things happened to show me that there was a better way. First, I enrolled Robin in a Montessori school. The activities of the youngest children in the school opened my eyes. The boys

Introduction

and girls were equally engrossed in wiping tables, cutting carrots, slicing bananas, washing dishes, and all the chores I typically thought of as "woman's work." Having never read Betty Friedan's *Feminine Mystique*, this was a new awareness for me. Could George and the kids share the load at home?

Second, I enrolled myself in an informal woman's group. The group had no name, but its purpose was to explore the concerns and directions of women in Cincinnati. We discussed life planning, career development, personal potential, and all sorts of heady things I'd never considered. As might have been predicted, I began to change my perception of my world and my life as wife and mother.

There I was, shedding my shell, just like a lobster, and it was scary. Everyone around me seemed to want a piece of me. My husband still wanted his meals on time, my kids wanted to be chauffeured everywhere, friends told me I was insane to rock the boat, and the school pressures were building. But the women in our group provided the support I needed to continue my resolve. So, despite much trauma, our family made it through the year.

I achieved success with my LD students at school, but the most interesting part of my job was counseling the parents on how to handle their kids at home. It turned out to be an eye opener for me, since the problems I heard from the mothers of these kids were the same ones I was hearing in my women's group—frustrations of motherhood, unrest, lack of emotional support, and guilt for these feelings.

Our women's group, meanwhile, became more formalized. What started out as a group of fifteen women meeting to discuss their own goals turned into a fully incorporated adult education corporation—Women Into Tomorrow (WIT). The members included an artist, a former nun, a social worker, a church leader, some women from the YWCA, some Junior Leaguers, some mental health volunteers, and several housewives. Our objective was to help women define their life goals. We were trained to offer life-planning programs patterned after the highly successful

Introduction

"Investigation Into Identity" program at Oakland University in Rochester, Michigan.

Helping women to better understand themselves and others was challenging. Now I had a whole cluster of lobsters shedding their shells and saying things that showed they were looking at themselves for the first time: "Before the women's movement, I never expected to be anything but a wife and mother"; "It's scary to think about change"; "Why do I feel so ambivalent?" I really felt a new purpose in life. I had my master's degree. Everything was coming together.

Right?

Wrong!

George decided that this was a terrific time to shed *his* shell. Successful Prince George, a conservative Proctor & Gamble marketing executive, announced it was time for a career change and a move to Lotus Land. My analytical mind told me it was a last-ditch effort to bring me back into the fold as a wife, mother, and suburban lady—we were even looking at a station wagon for our trip west! So, in July of 1973, I found myself in Palos Verdes, California . . . back in my shell and back in the suburbs. The "Summer of '73" had all the ingredients of a bad movie. The weather was cold and gray, nothing at all like the paradise George had promised. The kids and I were suffering transplant shock, and I was resisting the pressure to become a suburban housewife again. My neighbors encouraged me to volunteer in the school library, join the PTA, get into tennis doubles, sign my kids up for lessons and car pools, and I could feel the sensation of being pulled back into the old routine. Maybe George was right . . . I should be happy. Look at everything I had! But that was a trap, and I had to reach out to find something more.

I kept thinking of the song from *Inside Daisy Clover:* "Move over sun and give me some sky . . . I've got me some wings I'm eager to try, I may be unknown, but wait till I'm grown. . . . You're gonna hear from me!" I knew that singing wouldn't cure my depression, but the words inspired me to push ahead.

Introduction

> PROBLEM: depression . . . desperation
> SOLUTION: a job . . . any job

With a new master's degree in special education, I began a frenetic search for jobs that didn't exist. Unfortunately, there was a teacher surplus in California, and the only position I could find was as a part-time substitute speech therapist. With extra time on my hands, I painted the inside of my house manic colors: orange, yellow, purple, and red. When I ran out of walls, I painted doors.

Meanwhile, I had told everyone I met of my interest and experience in counseling and running women's life-planning groups in Ohio. One new friend said, "You ought to talk to Randi Gunther. She's really into running groups."

The minute I met Randi, I recognized another lobster who had shed many shells on her way to maturity. She was a graduate student getting a degree in marriage and family counseling after starting college as a thirty-five-year-old freshman. She'd given up college to put her husband through school, and now with three children almost grown, it was time for her. We hit it off immediately and decided to offer a life-planning awareness program for women in Palos Verdes.

> PROBLEM: good program . . . but nobody knew about it
> SOLUTION: publicity

We arranged for an interview with the *Peninsula News*, and the reporter we talked with was as excited about our project as we were. She arranged for us to have a full-page article in the profile section of the paper. We were off and running!

I remember our first group: fourteen women willing to be our guinea pigs for $35 apiece. I was frightened that someone would cry, crack up, or fall apart, and I didn't know if I could handle it. I didn't know Randi very well, and I didn't have the professional back-up I'd had in Cincinnati.

Introduction

Despite these fears, the group was a success. The effects of raised expectations were very noticeable. The women began to value themselves more, and their developing self-confidence was a first step toward taking responsibility for their own lives. Three of these women now have businesses of their own; four went back to school and got their degrees; one got married; and many began to openly communicate with their families to try and change unhappy situations at home.

Randi and I found that we were a terrific team. "Sandi and Randi" sounded like a vaudeville team, and in some respects the notion was appropriate. We both loved the role of the stand-up comic, and we made education both informative and delightfully entertaining.

Word of mouth spread the news about our work, and soon we were running two groups a week. The women in our programs came from diverse backgrounds: married, single, divorced, widowed, working, or at home with kids. But all were searching for more purpose in their lives. Some couldn't understand the purpose of the women's movement and had never felt disadvantaged as women, but most were discovering how narrow their lives had been and were eager to discover new options for themselves. On some days many of the women felt confusion, uncertainty, anger, or fear, and yet, on other days they felt that life was pretty much OK. The feelings of ambivalence were shared by all members, as they voiced their expectations for the program.

I remember wondering: Where am *I* going with this? What will be *my* next steps? Here I was teaching women how to set goals and I didn't know what my own next steps would be; but I knew I wanted something more. I too was growing daily in self-confidence, and it became apparent that to reach a wider audience I would have to go outside Palos Verdes.

> PROBLEM: expansion . . . small community, and we were running out of interested women
> SOLUTION: Los Angeles . . . UCLA Extension

Introduction

I remember telling a friend who'd lived in Los Angeles all her life that I would like to offer our program through UCLA Extension, and she said, "They already have too many programs for women, don't bother." But I felt that none could be the same as ours, or as good, so I made an appointment with Sallie O'Neill, coordinator of Women's Programs for UCLA Extension. Wonder of wonders, she agreed! Randi and I were asked to plan a new program to be called The Emerging Woman . . . Who do you think you are . . . and what are you going to do about it? George said we should set the title to music and offer it to Gladys Knight and the Pips. Nevertheless, that title attracted more than two hundred women to the program in the course of two years. There was even talk of turning it into a program for public broadcasting.

During a group discussion in the UCLA class, a student asked, "What if my husband won't let me go back to school?" I answered, "Some of the techniques you'll learn in this class will help you adjust to and cope with the new demands your family will make on you as you change your behavior." I made it all sound so easy. But it was true that George, Mr. Success, was learning to treat "Sandi Success" differently. No longer was I the "little woman." When my earnings began to pay for furniture, clothes, and vacations, he stopped considering my work a hobby. I too was finally able to let go of feeling guilty for doing something for myself. The phone calls from neighbors informing me that my children were actually walking home from a tennis lesson and didn't I think it was too cold and dark for them to walk no longer made me defensive. I remember saying, "Well, if you think so, give them a ride." And I meant it. I was letting the children take responsibility, and even they began to "honor their mother" and not expect her at their beck and call. The classes reinforced the idea that the risks were worth it. My fear that George might find another woman who'd be happy to fold his socks didn't materialize, and my children didn't become delinquents. Instead, I watched them become daily more self-reliant.

But I was still restless. And then the solution came from a

Introduction

department store. No, I didn't turn into a compulsive shopper. Rather, the Broadway Department Stores wanted to develop some programs of interest to women. The Broadway thought a seminar that would help women reenter the job market would be a big draw for them. Thus, the H.E.L.P. seminars were born. I was invited to be a speaker at these meetings and in the course of a year, I spoke to thousands of women at fourteen locations ranging from San Diego to the San Fernando Valley.

The message I delivered to these women—housewives, students, former secretaries, and nurses—makes up a great deal of what is to follow in these pages. The H.E.L.P. acronym letters stand for: *H*ow to find your place in the job market. *E*valuate your potential. *L*eave your anxieties behind. *P*repare for what's ahead.

There I was, lecturing for the Broadway Department Stores and running groups for UCLA Extension. What more could I want? I was feeling great and getting the satisfaction of motivating women and watching them change their lives.

Through UCLA, I met Elaine Wegener, a full-time personnel consultant, wife, and mother. We became friendly and she introduced me to other businesswomen. Gradually I became aware that women in business had problems of their own, and I could see the need for career development-life planning programs for businesswomen. As Elaine and I talked, I could feel my shell beginning to crack again . . . a new entrepreneurial career phase was beginning to take shape. I too could be a personnel consultant. I would offer my programs to help industry utilize the woman power at its disposal. The promise of doing something I loved and the prospects of greater financial reward spurred me on. Besides, Randi was now in private practice as a marriage and family counselor and was also a Ph.D. student; her time was much more limited. I knew it was time to strike out on my own.

Contacts, resources, organizations all began to have a business purpose for me. The women I'd met through Elaine were very supportive of my plans to offer programs in industry and

Introduction

many of them were in positions to help make that happen. My first clients came from that circle of friends.

It was 1975, and I was in business for myself as a personnel consultant to Twentieth-Century Fox, Systems Development Corporation, the Broadway Department Stores, and Personnel Women of Los Angeles. I remember picking up my stationery, Sandra Winston Associates, and feeling very proud.

My client list today is quite respectable. I offer career development, life-planning, and communication programs as part of a total management-development package. My programs are offered to managers, support staff, and new employees. They are no longer just something for the "girls" in the typing pool. They are for men and women alike and are accepted as business-related and valuable to the organization.

My counseling skills, education, and experience helped me to earn a license as a marriage and family counselor, and private practice is another option open to me as my shell gets ready to fall away again. Right now, the shell is beginning to get tight once more as I enter a new phase as writer, lecturer, and businesswoman. I don't know what this book will do for my career, but I believe it can help you develop the skills and insights necessary as you take the steps to become an entrepreneurial woman.

If it seems to you a long way from Cincinnati housewife to the entrepreneurial woman lunching at the Palm in New York, you're right. In the pages that follow, you'll read what it takes to make that journey on your own, how to get started, where the traps are, where to get help, the questions to ask, and how others like you have done it.

Note: some names and locations have been changed by request to protect the identities of the modest and the tax evaders. In some instances I have merged two personalities into one in the interest of brevity, but without the loss of authenticity.

$$$$$$$$ 1 $$$$$$$$
Entrepreneurship... is it for you?

Once I had set out I was already far on my way.
—Colette

So you're thinking of starting your own business? Great! But, before you pick out the drapes for your office or rent your store, there a few important questions you should ask yourself. Questions like who you really are, why you want to go into business, and do you have what it takes?

In this chapter, we'll take a look at the characteristics that most entrepreneurs share, characteristics that experts in the field believe are necessary if you are to turn your idea into a profit-making, rewarding endeavor.

Much research has been done in this field. MBA theses and doctoral dissertations have been written on what it takes. Dr. Albert Shapero, professor of management at the University of Texas Graduate School of Business has refined some significant theories. Dr. David McClelland of Harvard has studied entrepreneurship in developing nations and has written a definitive book on the subject of motivation and entrepreneurial activity. The Small Business Administration (SBA) has an awesome list of characteristics and traits that you need to be a successful entrepreneur. And, if you ask seventeen entrepreneurs what it takes, you'll get seventeen answers. You'll hear rules like:

"Ability to get along with people."
"High energy level and good health."

The Entrepreneurial Woman

"Creativity."

"A rich aunt in Milwaukee."

"Strong desire to achieve."

"You've got to be organized."

"You need a business background, and an MBA if possible."

"Parents who've had their own business."

"Experience in the kind of business you're starting."

"Confidence, independence, and self-reliance."

"Patience."

"Impatience."

"Sincerity and honesty."

"Ruthlessness . . . it's a cutthroat world out there."

And on and on until you feel so confused you don't know what to believe. The most thoughtful observers of the field have narrowed the list of contradictory and complex factors down to six. These include intangible traits, tangible resources, and circumstances. Let's look at each of these. They are, quite simply:

1. A feeling of displacement
2. Control: Do you have internal or external control over your destiny?
3. A feeling of independence
4. Role models
5. A willingness to take risks
6. The resources to make it happen

What if you're independent, displaced, self-motivated, but you're not a gambler? Don't pack up your dreams just yet. You can learn to fill in the blanks and acquire whatever it is that you

Entrepreneurship ... is it for you?

may need in order to enter the entrepreneurial ranks.

We owe a debt of gratitude here to the experts and the SBA for their research on entrepreneurship. Unfortunately, most of their research on the subject has been with men. In this chapter, we'll look at how these factors affect women as well.

A man is displaced when he's fired, transferred, or his company moves. Women can be displaced when this happens to them or their husbands, when they are divorced, widowed or separated, when their kids grow up, or if their current jobs turn sour. Successful men understand what it means to be in control, to take charge. Many women have never been in charge of much more than car-pool arrangements and shopping lists. The same applies to the issue of independence. You'll read how one woman almost lost her entire sense of independence because of marriage and how it took a journey to snap her back to where she was fourteen years earlier. Finally, many women, single and married, feel that gambling and taking risks is inconsistent with the role society has imposed on them. But you need to take chances to go into business for yourself.

So you see, women have special and unique circumstances that can either help or hinder them in their efforts to become entrepreneurs. The first step is to recognize these circumstances and turn them to your advantage.

A FEELING OF DISPLACEMENT

Nancy wanted to go back to work and thought she'd return to teaching when her kids were older. She knew jobs were scarce, but she figured that with a little more education it would be easy to become a reading specialist or special-education teacher. WRONG! Teaching used to be "something to fall back on when the kids are grown," but now even teachers are becoming displaced persons. Nancy found that school systems were cutting back even on special teachers. So, with no chance of a job in her

The Entrepreneurial Woman

chosen field, Nancy was feeling lost. She had a clear goal of wanting to work with children, a love of reading, and a little bit of money stashed away, left from her grandmother's estate. She thought of opening a children's bookstore, but on closer investigation found it would take more money than she had. After a lot more thinking, she arrived at a creative solution. She would open a children's reading and play section in an existing local independent bookstore. All she had to do was convince the owner.

It took her a few months to get to know the owner well enough to broach the subject. Then they agreed to a "trial marriage." Nancy worked in the shop as an employee for three months before the owner was ready to accept her idea. Now, Nancy has expanded the business, has a piece of the action, and has realized her goal of working with children.

Transplant shock is another displacing factor for women in today's society. How many of us have moved around the country because our husband's careers have taken us to a different city every few years?

I remember waking up one morning in California with a start. Where was I? This didn't look like my bedroom in Cincinnati. Where was the navy blue wallpaper? Where were my corner windows? What were those beams doing in my ceiling?

I was lost! A refugee in a foreign land. I was a displaced person—not only because I was living in California but also because I was a thirty-five-year-old housewife with no real future. Why was I so depressed? Transplant shock takes some time to get over, but I knew I had to do something soon or else sink deeper into the morass. Being displaced does strange things. You begin to recognize that you don't have your usual supports around you—supports like friends, family, and such—and you soon come to the realization that you have only yourself to rely on.

The same thing happened to our foremothers and forefathers when they came to these shores. In my childhood neighborhood, Chicago in the late '40s, there were many family businesses—grocery stores, tailors, restaurants, butcher shops, dress shops.

Entrepreneurship ... is it for you?

Many of the owners were displaced persons who had arrived in Chicago fleeing Hitler. These D.P.s had settled in my neighborhood and started "mom and pop" businesses. It was the only thing they could do; it was a fresh start. Even the Chinese restaurant on the corner was owned by a refugee family that had emigrated from Hong Kong.

That's how I was feeling in California. I wasn't running from oppression, but it still seemed as though I'd have to make a job for myself. Everyone else in the family was getting into her or his own thing. The kids had school, George had a new job—and I had the same old castle in the suburbs. It was time for me to get going.

I wondered how many women felt this sense of displacement as they made the decision to do something new in their lives. I began to ask questions of the women I met who also had started businesses in the past few years.

I talked to Randi, whose girls were all of college age now. She'd gone back to school for the college education she'd given up to become a wife and mother. As her kids grew up, she began to feel a real sense of loss, a sense of displacement. She told me the only way she had been able to "find" herself again was to develop her own interests and get recognition outside the home. She'd done the volunteer thing, sold artwork from her home, been a car-pool mother for the neighborhood dance classes, and even come up with some toy ideas that she'd sold to a local manufacturer. None of this was enough for her.

She set out to become a psychotherapist. She told me she'd always been a psychotherapist—but this time she wanted to be legitimate. What she meant, of course, was that everyone had always come to her with their problems since she'd been a little girl, but now she wanted the credentials to become a licensed professional and get paid for her skills and efforts. Her feeling of displacement was the first thing that pushed her to develop her skills and get the necessary schooling. Today, Randi is close to obtaining her Ph.D., is a licensed psychotherapist in California, and has her own private counseling practice.

The Entrepreneurial Woman

Helen, too, was feeling a great sense of displacement because of a recent mastectomy. Her sense of herself as a woman was tremendously threatened, and the psychological stress of being less than whole was affecting her deeply. She'd been an active businesswoman her whole life, but illness and family considerations had caused her to turn her business over to others. Now she was faced with a lot of free time, an active brain, and the knowledge that there were no jobs for a woman of her experience, background, age, and physical condition. However, researching a new business began to energize her . . . gave her a new sense of her own worth. And before she knew it, she was back in business, manufacturing a product that was her own idea.

Empty nest, moving to a new state, illness, changing job market, what are the other displacing factors that influence women's lives?

Think about divorce and the growing belief in the courts that women now can and in many cases do earn as much as men. "Alimony" is becoming a dirty word. So, what's a woman with two small children, no recent work history, child-care problems, and no alimony to do? Many of the divorced women I met had no thought of going into business before their marriages broke up, but now many were running businesses from their homes. One has gone into the catering business, specializing in party planning, another gives French lessons in her home, a third offers belly-dancing classes in her garage. Conducting exercise or yoga classes, producing personal astrology charts, doing graphoanalysis, making ceramic bowls and planters—all these and many more are some of the businesses divorced women run from their homes.

Carole decided to begin an interior design business from her home. Her children were one and three years old, she was a recent divorcee, and she'd worked for an interior design firm before her marriage. As her business grew, she soon had four assistants, and her living room looked like a disaster area. *Better*

Entrepreneurship ... is it for you?

Homes and Gardens would never shoot this layout for its pages on glorious home offices. Desks and papers everywhere ... four phones ... and in the midst of it all, tricycles, cap guns, and mountains of other kiddy litter lying around. Carole's move from her home into a real office was prompted by another act of displacement ... but this time it was the Beverly Hills police who wanted to displace her! There's a law against operating a business in your home in Beverly Hills. More about Carole later.

Are you feeling displaced as you read this chapter? If so, remember that this feeling might be the internal push you need to get out there and do something for yourself. It's pushed hundreds of others. Displacement can become a real energizer if only you'll let it.

Run through the checklist below to learn if you qualify as a D.P.

$$

D. P. CHECKLIST

Have you recently moved to a new city or neighborhood?

Are your kids growing up and leaving home?

Are you too old to get the job you want?

Are you recently divorced or widowed?

Is the job market in your chosen field overcrowded?

Did your best friend just get a job, leaving you with no one to "play" with?

Are you fed up with what you're doing now?

Is your term as head of an exciting volunteer project over?

Have you recently quit or been fired from a job?

Are you in a dead-end job?

Has an illness left you "unemployable"?

$$

The Entrepreneurial Woman

If you answered "Yes" to any of the above questions, then you're a genuinely displaced person, one of the most important circumstances leading to entrepreneurship.

OK, now you've got a name for what you're feeling. You thought it was "depressed." Well now, doesn't "displaced" sound more uplifting? You know you want to do something, you're beginning to realize that the something will have to be self-motivated, so let's look at what really turns you on.

CONTROL:
DO YOU HAVE INTERNAL OR
EXTERNAL CONTROL OVER YOUR DESTINY?

Do you have the motivation and determination to go into business for yourself? Do you feel you truly can do it? Are you the kind who decides you're going to do something and goes ahead and does it? Or, do you wait around for the friend who will promise to join you on your adventure? What turns you on? Is it your own inner need to do something, to be in control? Or, is it the external motivators of friends, husband, children, mother, newspapers, TV, magazines, or the fact that everyone else is "doing something"? Did you take up tennis because it was the thing to do, or because you wanted to learn the game, to do well, and even to WIN?

How does that word sound? "WIN, WIN, WIN." It's a word that energizes the born entrepreneur with inner feelings of push and drive. Most entrepreneurs are controlled, even driven, by the inner need to succeed, to accomplish, to win. They are influenced but are hardly ever controlled by outside forces.

Elaine Wegener was displaced. After being squeezed out of a consulting firm she helped start, she spent a year working from her home as a freelance consultant. She had been in the business world for years, and she needed to feel she was again part of the action and give-and-take in a firm. She knew she had what it takes

Entrepreneurship ... is it for you?

to succeed in business. It was scary starting her own firm, but she didn't let fear stop her. Once she had made up her mind to do it, Elaine found three partners and sold them on the idea of going into business. She knew the odds were against her . . . every other consultant she talked with told her of the failure rate. But she didn't let their "wisdom" stand in her way either. She rented space in a large downtown office building, agreed with her partners to forego salary for the better part of that first year, and went after clients.

Right from the start she was clearly in charge. She knew her future was on the line and she acted. She was willing to take risks, work hard, be an aggressive go-getter, and she did so without compromising her femininity. That's where you can see Elaine's inner controls in operation. She didn't let the opinions of others stand in her way. Two years later, her firm, PACT, was going strong—her gross sales increasing substantially every year.

Are you frightened of being known as an aggressive businesswoman? Are you worried about what people will say if you push for the best deal? Do you think people will think less of you? If these old tapes are still playing in your brain, be aware that they may very well hold you back in the business world.

Where are you on the continuum of feelings of control? Go over the following checklist to see where you stand.

$$$

CHECKLIST FOR INTERNAL
OR EXTERNAL FEELINGS OF CONTROL

1. Do you often feel "That's just the way things are, and there's nothing I can do about it"? ____Yes____No
2. When things go right and are terrific for you, do you think, "It's mostly luck!"? ____Yes____No

The Entrepreneurial Woman

3. Do you think you "should" go into business or do something with your time for pay because everything you read these days is urging you in that direction?
   ____Yes____No

4. Do you know that if you decide to do something, you'll do it and nothing can stop you? ____Yes____No

5. Even though it's scary to try something new, are you the kind who tries it? ____Yes____No

6. Your friends, husband, and mother tell you that it's foolish of you to want a career. Have you listened to them and stayed home all these years? ____Yes____No

7. Do you think it's important for everyone to like you? ____Yes____No

8. When you do a good job, is your pleasure in a job well done satisfaction enough? ____Yes____No

9. If you want something, do you ask for it rather than wait for someone to notice you and "just give it to you"? ____Yes____No

10. Even though people tell you "it can't be done," do you have to find out for yourself? ____Yes____No

$$$

If you answered Yes to questions 4, 5, 8, 9, and 10, you seem to have the internal control necessary for entrepreneurship. Yes to questions 1, 2, 3, 6, and 7 indicates external controls are holding you back.

It's fairly easy to tell from the preceding list whether you're the kind of person who's driven from the inside or held back from the outside. Tied very closely to feelings of control are feelings for independence. Maybe you thought you could do anything when you were eighteen, even leap over buildings in a single bound! What's happened to that confident inner person of the past? Can you resurrect her?

INDEPENDENCE
(or "Please, Mother, I'd rather do it myself!")

Most of us who are mothers know what it's like when the two-year-old begins to feel independent. It's the "No" and the pulling away from you as you're crossing the street. We all went through this stage with our kids, and our mothers before us went through it with us. But a lot of us have become pretty dependent beings through the years. What happened?

A Columbus, Ohio woman told me she'd been invited to join her husband on a Florida business trip. At the last minute his plans were changed and he had to go via New York. They couldn't afford her expenses for that leg of the trip, so he assumed she'd have to skip the entire trip. She hadn't traveled alone since they were married twelve years before, and he knew how nervous she was about flying. To say that she was paralyzed by her fear is an understatement: she had forgotten how to leave the car at the airport, how to get her bags to the check-in counter, how to get someone to carry her bags, how much to tip, how to find the right plane, and even what to do when she got off the plane at the other end.

Her friends were no help. They told her to stay home! Without her husband, how would she ever get from the Miami airport to her hotel in Key Biscayne, and what would she do when she got there? He wouldn't get there till the next day.

She told me that this experience was the turning point in her life. She suddenly realized, to her horror, that the confident girl of eighteen who felt she could travel around the world alone had become the woman of thirty-two who had allowed herself to become so dependent upon her husband that without him she was helpless. This revelation drove her into action. She forced herself to go. In Miami she rented a car, read maps like a grownup, and found the hotel. It was not, however, entirely successful. When she got to the hotel, people were sitting around the pool, and she in her paranoia thought that everyone would

The Entrepreneurial Woman

wonder what she was doing by herself in a place like that. So she allowed her fear to get the best of her, and she spent the afternoon and evening in her room with the TV and room service.

That experience awakened her to the realization that she had lost her ability to function as an independent person. She determined to find her old sense of inner control and bring it to the surface. Today, eight years later, this same woman owns her own business, travels alone, goes into restaurants alone without feeling self-conscious. Once the feeling of independence emerges, there's no putting it down, and research bears this out. Successful entrepreneurs more often than not are independent and self-reliant. They know it's not luck, but hard work, determination, and their own need to achieve that pushes them into entrepreneurship and keeps them there.

Are you a person who wants to do it your way, in your own time and in a place of your own choosing? Look at the following checklist to see if you're the independent kind. Looking at the word "independence," you can see how closely it is tied to inner dependence or control.

$$

CHECKLIST FOR FEELINGS OF INDEPENDENCE

1. I hate to go shopping for clothes alone.   ____Yes____No
2. If my friends won't go to a movie I want to see, I'll go by myself.   ____Yes____No
3. I want to be financially independent.   ____Yes____No
4. I often need to ask other people's opinions before I decide on important things.   ____Yes____No
5. I'd rather have other people decide where to go on a social evening out.   ____Yes____No

Entrepreneurship ... is it for you?

6. When I know I'm in charge, I don't apologize, I just do what has to be done. ____Yes____No
7. I'll speak up for an unpopular cause if I believe in it. ____Yes____No
8. I'm afraid to be different. ____Yes____No
9. I want the approval of others. ____Yes____No
10. I usually wait for people to call me to go places, rather than intrude on them. ____Yes____No

$$

Yes answers to items 1, 4, 5, 8, 9, and 10 would indicate you need to work on developing your own sense of independence more fully in order to compete in the business world.

Linda Cannon is the epitome of an independent woman. One day she decided she was going to Europe to buy antiques. Nobody could tell her not to go; she had made up her mind. So she found a university group going to London on an antique-buying and educational junket. She signed up and took off. It helped, of course, to have a mother who would watch the kids and a husband so busy he hardly knew she was gone.

Linda's friends had tried to dissuade her: "What do you know about importing antiques?" ... "It'll cost so much money" ... "How will you know they're real?" ... "You'll lose a lot of money" ... "Who'll buy what you don't use?" ... "How will you pay for your trip?" ... "Your husband will be angry, do you want to take that chance?" ... "He'll probably have an affair while you're away." In the face of these and various other "supportive" statements designed to keep her in her place, she became even more determined to go. She carried herself beyond just thinking independently, she moved into action. What was Linda's secret? INDEPENDENCE ... it makes all the difference. (P.S. The antiques Linda bought and subsequently sold more than

The Entrepreneurial Woman

paid for her trip and helped her start her own antique business.)

Jackie, on the other hand, found she couldn't operate independently as a photographer. She teamed up with a friend who was supposed to do the selling, handle the billing, and set up appointments. Jackie's plan was to show up and do the creative work photographing kids, dogs, weddings, bar mitzvahs, and parties. However, her friend, Harriet, was overcommitted and didn't get Jackie enough bookings. So what was Jackie to do? She recognized her weakness and her limitations and looked around for another activity in which she could use her talents but wouldn't have to be involved in the day-to-day selling and administrative headaches. She looked at who she was: displaced homemaker with two girls in school all day, wife of a corporate executive, former teacher, camp counselor. What did she like to do the most? She had always loved tennis. She not only liked it but was an "A" player. But how to turn tennis into a money-making venture, knowing she'd need some administrative backup? She decided to become an independent contractor and get someone else to organize the classes and keep the books. She was highly motivated, the need for achievement was there, the desire to earn her own money was there. The rest is history.

Jackie went to the local community center, told them her idea, and started that summer with a children's tennis program. Today, she is a tennis pro, established at an indoor court for the winter months and at an outdoor club for the summer months. When I last talked with her, she was working thirty hours a week, but planned her own hours. Her clients book through the clubs she has contracted with, the clubs handle the billing, and Jackie teaches. She has found her own level of independence.

ROLE MODELS

You read so much these days about women needing role models and/or mentors to become successful in the business world. It's

Entrepreneurship ... is it for you?

true even for entrepreneurs. Often, entrepreneurship seems to be inbred. It is learned, so to speak, at Mom's and Dad's knees—especially Dad's. The old expression, "like father, like son," seems to apply to a great extent to male entrepreneurs. How many men do you know today who went into "Dad's" business? On the other hand, how few women go into "Mom's" business? So, where do we get our role models? And without role models, how do we really picture ourselves as credible businesswomen?

Maybe you know someone who went into his dad's business and you can say to yourself, "If that dumb * * * can be a successful businessperson, so can I." Or, maybe you worked for someone, held down the shop in his absence, and knew you could do it better than he. Well, that's a role model of sorts. Sometimes this kind of negative role model can be more of an incentive than a positive role model. One of the most successful theatrical agents I know started as a secretary to a mediocre but successful male agent. She saw him operate, faults and all, and figured that if he could do it, so could she. She was right!

Whitney Backlar's role model was her mother—yes, here's one daughter who learned success at her mother's knees. Mother was a very well-known West Coast interior designer, and Whitney grew up knowing she was the daughter of a special person. Some kids might crumple under that pressure, but Whitney proved herself in another field. She played out the typical story of wanting to establish her independence, and she made her mark as a highly paid fashion model in New York and Europe. She soon tired of that work, however, and came back home to join her mother's firm as an interior designer. She's now running her own firm, designing furniture and fabrics as well as interiors. Having Mom for a role model taught her a lot about the realities of the business world, and she's one of the best young businesswomen I know. She learned the value of her time early, saw that artistic talent can be turned into big business, and has few hangups about demanding money for her design work.

What if you don't have an obvious role model? Can you still

The Entrepreneurial Woman

carry on as an independent businesswoman? The answer is "Yes!" After you begin, you may find you have a role model that you hadn't even thought about.

I was already engaged in consulting before I realized that I had picked up a lot of my know-how listening to my Dad talk about his work as a production manager in a small manufacturing company. I never made the connection until he asked me one day, "How do you know about production and cost controls?" I was then conducting a time-management training program in a manufacturing concern.

I said, "I don't know, seems I just picked it up somewhere. Most of it's good common sense anyway."

My Dad, who's now retired, gently reminded me of what I'd heard around the house when I was growing up and he was studying time and motion engineering. It all came back to me . . . the leaf doesn't fall that far from the tree! Even though he'd been a corporate being, he was entrepreneurial in his own way—and this daughter had followed in his footsteps. I'd had a hidden role model.

You may have a role model who's not in business but can make an impact on your life. Eleanor Driver, who was the director of the Continuum Center at Michigan's Oakland University, had an impact on many women's lives, including mine. When I met Eleanor, she was a fifty-nine-year-old reentry woman whom I saw as a typical suburban mother who'd done all the right things as her kids were growing up. She was now a widow with three grown sons and a completely changed life. As the leader of our "Investigation into Identity" group, she was completely enthusiastic. I thought, "She's so groovy for her age." The story of how she had changed careers in midlife encouraged many other women to get their lives moving again. I know she gave me courage!

As we grow and our goals change, we may meet other people who will serve as our role models, even mentors. Some may be negative role models, people who seem less qualified or

Entrepreneurship ... is it for you?

not as smart as us, and we think, "If they can sell their act, so can I." You may even have to serve as your own role model sometimes. When confronted with a new and scary situation, you may need to be able to imagine how the "you within" (remember the confident eighteen-year-old) would handle it. Think about how you conquered that last obstacle, your last success experience, and you'll be your own role model. What a great feeling! And it becomes even more exciting each time you try and succeed.

Who are your role models? Look over the following checklist and see what you come up with.

$$$

ROLE MODEL CHECKLIST

1. Did your grandparents come to this country in the last century? ____Yes____No
2. Did they own their own business? ____Yes____No
3. Did you grow up in a neighborhood where there were a lot of family-owned, small businesses? ____Yes____No
4. Do you have a friend in business for herself?
 ____Yes____No
5. Was one of your parents in business for him/herself?
 ____Yes____No
6. Was one of your parents an independent professional; that is, doctor, lawyer, dentist, tutor, psychologist, etc.?
 ____Yes____No
7. Were you, as a youngster, a person who was always starting things; that is, did you organize clubs, the neighborhood plays, lemonade stands, charity drives, etc.? ____Yes____No

The Entrepreneurial Woman

    8. Is your husband in business for himself? ____Yes____No
    9. Can you imagine yourself as an independent business person? ____Yes____No
   10. Can you imagine what an average day would be like with you at the head of your own business?
                                                 ____Yes____No

$$

If your answers to any of the above questions are Yes, you've got a role model. Questions 1, 2, 3, 5, and 6 relate to whether or not you experienced an entrepreneurial environment when you were growing up. Research seems to indicate that those people who did tend to believe in the credibility of becoming entrepreneurs. Questions 7, 9, and 10 relate to you being your own role model.

A WILLINGNESS TO TAKE RISKS

Judy, whose husband is a successful literary agent, knows what's involved in setting up a business as an independent professional. She's seen the pressures of getting clients and setting up and running a business. Now she's ready to open her own law firm after recycling herself from a career as a teacher and mother into one as an attorney. She's worked for a law firm for the past two years, is one of a small number of women in the firm, and feels left out of the major decision-making process. She feels underutilized, displaced! She has an independent spirit, an excellent education, a client base, and a role model. She saw her husband build his business and knows if he could do it, so can she! She sees the opportunity to become her own boss as a golden one.

What do you see in the word "RISK"? The Chinese symbol for risk is a combination of the symbols for danger and opportunity. Do you see only the danger? Do the fears and the knowledge of business-failure rates overwhelm and immobilize you?

Entrepreneurship ... is it for you?

Going into business is risky. If you're married and have children, will you be able to find the time to provide the care your family needs? One thing that held Susan back for years was the fear that her teenagers would turn into pot-smoking juvenile delinquents if she devoted all of the necessary time to a business. When her sons began to smoke pot anyway, she figured she should have taken the risk. But at the time a 9 A.M.-3 P.M. teaching job seemed the safer way to go. She saw only the danger in the partnership that was offered to her, not the opportunity.

Risks concerning your family are only a part of those you'll face. What about the risk of losing the money you're going to invest in your business? There are no guarantees. Can you afford to lose it? The scorecard for business success isn't the greatest. About fifty-five percent of new businesses fail by the end of five years. Are you willing to risk that?

And finally, are you willing to risk success? If your business grows by leaps and bounds, creating even more demands on your time, will you risk ignoring old friends and even loved ones as you juggle your activities?

Linda's business grew so fast into a national venture that she found herself traveling around the country on promotional trips to department stores. In one year she scheduled fifty-eight trips. Her husband was beginning to feel neglected and became petulant. She recognized her success was having a negative effect on the relationship—but she wanted both her husband and her business.

She took the risk and plunged ahead with her travel schedule. Her husband still wasn't too happy, but her belief in herself paid off. Today, she doesn't have to travel as much and she has the proudest husband around—but all in all, as Linda admits, it was a difficult year.

How are you on risk-taking behavior? Look at the following checklist to find out.

$$$

CHECKLIST FOR
A WILLINGNESS TO TAKE RISKS

1. Can you take risks with money, that is, invest and not know the outcome? ____Yes____No

2. Do you take an umbrella with you every time you travel? A hot water bottle, a thermometer? ____Yes____No

3. If you're frightened of something, will you try to conquer the fear? ____Yes____No

4. Do you like trying new food, new places, and totally new experiences? ____Yes____No

5. Do you need to know the answer before you'll ask the question? ____Yes____No

6. Have you taken a risk in the last six months? ____Yes____No

7. Can you walk up to a total stranger and strike up a conversation? ____Yes____No

8. Have you ever intentionally traveled on an unfamiliar route? ____Yes____No

9. Do you need to know that it's been done already, before you're willing to try it? ____Yes____No

10. Have you ever gone on a blind date? ____Yes____No

$$$

Yes answers to questions 2, 5, and 9 indicate you may need to work to develop stronger willingness to take risks.

What if you don't check out as a risk-taking person? Can you do anything about it? The answer is YES, most emphatically! You can train yourself in risk-taking behavior. How? you might ask. The answer is BEGIN! Take a small risk today, do something that

Entrepreneurship ... is it for you?

scares you a little. See how it feels. What's the worst thing that happens to you? You'll read more about how to develop your self-confidence and risk-taking behavior in the following chapters of the book.

In this chapter we've considered the "who" and the "why" aspects of entrepreneurship ... Is it for you? We've considered the "where" as it applies to feeling displaced. You've had a chance to look at yourself in terms of independence, risk taking, and role models. The final factor common to all successful entrepreneurship is the availability of resources. Resources are so important they deserve a chapter of their own.

$$$$$$$ 2 $$$$$$$$

Entrepreneurship ... do you have the resources?

Nothing great was ever achieved without enthusiasm.
—Ralph Waldo Emerson

You've gone through the checklists in the preceding chapter and decided you've got what it takes to be an entrepreneur. You've even got what you think is a great idea for making lots of money. On top of that, you've got chutzpah, energy, and drive. So what else do you need? Plenty!

For sure you'll need money to get going. How much depends on the nature of your business. But just as important as money is time and your other resources: your own inner assets, interests, likes and dislikes, your contacts for information, even your ideas and personal needs. How many businesses have started because the owner had a personal need, guessed that others shared that need, and found the courage to fill that need in the marketplace?

This chapter will identify the resources you might need and help you to understand the resources you already have.

TAKING STOCK OF YOURSELF

You are the best resource you'll ever have, and here's why. You have the enthusiasm and eagerness to succeed, and you have your learning and experience to back you up. Maybe you've spent the last several years in a job that is going nowhere. Even if that is the case, look at what you've learned and what you've

The Entrepreneurial Woman

done. You've had to meet demands and commitments, you've had responsibility and challenge (at least when the job was new), you've matured, and with maturity comes better judgment.

"STOP," you may be saying, "I've been home raising a family for the past fifteen years, what experience do I have?" Are you trying to say that housewifery and mothering isn't a full-time job and a challenging experience? Not only did you have to organize your time, delegate authority, plan and budget, but you've also acted as chief counseling psychologist and personnel director in this small service-oriented business of the home. Now, what's that you were saying about lack of meaningful experience?

If you've been a volunteer outside the home, perhaps you've raised funds, planned luncheons and dinners for hundreds of people, done PR and sales marketing in the community, and had experience ranging from the administrative to the executive. If your recent work history wasn't salaried, look at it this way: you've *already* been your own boss. In child rearing you've learned to listen to your own feelings and trust your common sense no matter what the experts said. Well, you'll need that same intuitive knowledge in your own business.

What are your special needs? Do they tie in with your experience and talent? Can they be put together to form the basis for a business?

Ruth Handler had a special need. After her mastectomy, she couldn't locate a prosthesis anywhere at any price that fit properly or looked well under her clothes. Since Ruth was president of Mattel, the toy company she and her husband had founded, her public appearances were numerous, and her personal appearance was extremely important to her. In her typical manner, she decided that if what she wanted wasn't available, she would make it herself. After much trial and error, she designed a custom prosthesis that met her needs.

Ruth knew that if she had this need, there must be thousands

Do you have the resources?

of other women who shared it. After her retirement from Mattel, she formed the Ruthton Corporation to fill that need. "Nearly Me," the artificial breast prosthesis she manufactures, comes in 70-80 sizes, both right and left models, and is now available in department and specialty stores across the country. Out of her own personal trauma and need, a business was born. And to hear her tell it, it's given her a whole new purpose in life. She lights up when she talks about the women she has met who are thrilled with her product. She derives real joy from this mission, and at the age of sixty has found a new life for herself.

Barbara Davis-Venn had exquisite taste. She'd always had good fashion sense and design talent and even with limited funds could create a look in clothes or interior decor that had the polish of a Paris designer. She'd been a junior buyer in a large department store, but marriage and two daughters forced her to put career goals aside.

Because of her design talent, she was made the head of the decorations committee for a large charity ball in Cincinnati. She had a budget to work with and the design department of Pogue's Department Stores to assist her. She developed a professional working relationship with Pogue's designers, and her ideas influenced their work profoundly. She did such an outstanding job that she was asked to repeat it the next year. Again she worked with the design department of Pogue's. By now they respected her taste and ideas, and again the decor at the ball was breathtaking. Barbara had learned a lot in those two years. She learned she was an excellent manager and delegator. She had put her friends, family, and children to work for her, and had them up to their elbows in glue, feathers, and beads before they could protest. She had also learned how exhausting such a project can be. Therefore, after the charity work was done and she decided she would like to make decorative items for profit as well as fun, she already knew what she was getting into. Mexican paper flowers were the rage at that time, and Barbara soon cornered the market. Before any of her friends could discourage her she had a

The Entrepreneurial Woman

contract with Pogue's to supply paper flowers for its spring displays. One contract led to another, and soon Buds by Babs was a full-time business operating from Barbara's home.

She didn't earn a fortune, but she certainly learned about BUSINESS! From that venture she learned she had sales and organizational ability, and she developed the self-confidence to get involved in local community politics. She was elected president of the Clifton Town Council, worked on the better housing league, met the officials in Cincinnati's city hall, and made important contacts all over the city. She has put all that experience and ability to work today in a quasi-entrepreneurial venture as a director of Corporate Relocation, working with several large firms in Cincinnati. She's researching neighborhoods—the schools, shopping, churches, community organizations—and compiling this information for a major real estate agency. Her knowledge of the community and her contacts in city hall make the service she's providing uniquely hers.

Look at Barbara's story again. It's the story of an ordinary housewife who used her own resources, her hidden talents in volunteer activities, as a springboard to entrepreneurship.

Sheila O'Brien used her experience in the travel industry when she decided to open her own travel agency, Travel Designs, in Los Angeles. She'd been a flight attendant for Pan American for several years, and she could see her chances for advancement were limited. She loved to travel, but flying back and forth to Bangkok every week was becoming boring. As a flight attendant, she'd developed the confidence needed to relate to new people, places, and experiences, and she knew she was ready for a greater challenge. By knowing her strengths and understanding the positive aspects of her experience, she gained the courage necessary to begin. But she did have one problem—she had to have a steady income. It came down to this: how could she keep her job and start a business at the same time? Which brings us to the problem of time.

TIME AND COMMITMENT

Is this going to be a dilettante's venture, or is it what you want to do the rest of your life? If you're as serious as Sheila was, you're going to have to look at the amount of time you can devote to the business and fit this into your existing life schedule—or change that schedule.

Sheila O'Brien solved her problem that first year by continuing as a flight attendant but using her time between flights to research the field, ask questions about sites, financing, accreditation, staffing, and so on. She eventually selected her site, in Los Angeles' Pacific Design Center, named her business "Travel Designs," and started promoting it. Then she found someone she could work with to cover for her when she was off in the Far East. The area that suffered was her social life, but she was willing to give this up to get her business off the ground. An easy flight schedule and a sharply reduced social life gave Sheila the time she needed to start her own travel agency.

For Frad Young and Valerie Hartshorne, time was a precious commodity also. They wanted a business, but neither of them wanted to devote full time to it. They solved their problem with a restaurant, Soup du Jour, in Hopewell, New Jersey. Its menu is limited: soup, bread, and dessert. They're open only for lunch, three hours a day, and they cover for each other on their days off. They're both housewives and mothers and both continue to consider their families the major priority in their lives.

Absentee ownership is another way to buy time if you're presently holding down a full-time job. Barbara Sullivan is the personnel manager for an office of several hundred people. She has a special talent for handling people, and she realized she could put that talent to work for herself entrepreneurially. Since I've known Barbara she's been the owner of three businesses—a car wash, a boys' home, and a franchised diet program. She buys time by finding partners or managers to run her businesses. She's

The Entrepreneurial Woman

the first "moonlighting" woman I've met, but more and more women with well-paying jobs are going that route to achieve financial independence.

CONTACTS ... YOU NEED ALL KINDS

Everyone who's been interviewed for this book spoke of contacts of one type or another. Contacts are not just people who will "get it for you wholesale." They're people who might help you raise capital, tell you how much you'll need, maybe even loan you a few thousand. They're people who have "been there before" and can help keep you from making the same mistakes they've made. They'll save you a great deal of time as you search for the suppliers you'll need to make your business a going concern. They're a source of word-of-mouth advertising. In the beginning they're the people who can give you the kick in the pants to make you stick with it—and can help you over the rough spots.

When Frad and Valerie went into the restaurant business, they turned to a friend's husband for advice. He had been in the catering business and was able to give them information that saved them steps and time as they set up their "soup kitchen."

Judy needed contacts of a different kind; she needed suppliers for her discount boutique. She wanted to buy manufacturers' overproduction and offer it at a discount to her customers. But first she needed access to the manufacturers. Would they be willing to do business with her? Judy didn't let that question discourage her. She talked to her mother-in-law, Freida, who had had a ladies' dress shop for years. Sure enough, Freida was able to introduce Judy to the manufacturers she knew in Los Angeles, and before long Judy was using those manufacturing contacts to meet more manufacturers. Today, her store is stocked with the latest in junior fashions, all sold at discount prices.

If you don't have contacts, make them! Bunny Brow needed

Do you have the resources?

contacts to set up her interior design business in Palos Verdes Estates. She needed workers who could hang wallpaper for clients, refinish floors, reupholster furniture, build tables to specifications—people who could be counted on for good quality workmanship. While her business was growing, she set aside one day a week to make contacts and investigate the resources available in the city. She visited showrooms to learn who did their work for them; she went to manufacturers to find out if they did custom work. She called friends to see who had hung their wallpaper and what kind of a job they had done. Soon she had filled up her Rolodex with names of reliable people to help in her business.

Other business people can be a great source of information and expertise if you'll let them. How many of us have people close to us who would offer their expertise if they knew we needed it, if only we'd ask? When I started my consulting business, I was reluctant to use my husband's expertise even though he'd had fifteen years' more business experience than I.

I kept saying, "Please George, I'd rather do it myself."

I'd write business letters, proposals, make contacts, and try to sell my programs. I won some and lost some. When he asked how I was doing, I was evasive, and sometimes defensive. I needed to develop confidence in my own abilities before I could ask him for help and comments about the different aspects of my consulting business. In retrospect, waiting so long to use this resource at hand was a mistake. Don't make the same error.

Competition can also be a great resource for you. Once you recognize that it's a big world out there and that there will be room for you and your competitors, you'll be able to go to the other members of your chosen field for information.

Elaine and Sheila wanted to open a children's clothing store. One of the first persons they spoke to about their idea was the owner of a children's wear store in another neighborhood. That owner was very willing to share her knowledge and expertise

The Entrepreneurial Woman

with them. She told them honestly and candidly about the kind of inventory they'd have to carry, how much money they would need to set up shop, the kind of hours they would have to work, and how long it might take before the business would provide an adequate income. It took them about three months of information gathering, careful planning, site investigation, and soul searching to recognize that neither of them wanted to make the full-time commitment necessary for that business to work. Today, both of them are employed in secure jobs with a guaranteed income. Through the use of contacts, they were able to determine that the risk and time commitment ruled out that particular enterprise for them. As a result, they have no misgivings or regrets.

Looking at how independent professionals use contacts in business will provide you with role models for using other people in your own field. Most doctors and lawyers refer clients to their colleagues if they can't meet their needs. Word-of-mouth business development is a time-tested method of getting business. Are you embarrassed to let the owner of the dress store down the street know that you too might open a shop near hers? Look at it this way: if you contact her, let her know what type of merchandise you carry, and offer to refer customers for her specialties. Chances are you'll develop a profitable working relationship with a competitor.

It's a well-known fact that two gift stores or restaurants on a street will attract more traffic than one. If you want to open a small independent business, it might make sense to move next to a large chain store that sells similar merchandise and advertises heavily. Could you use that store's traffic and advertising as a contact to gain customers? You could if you were able to rent the space next door and merchandise competitively.

Making contacts with people in related fields can also pay off. The shop across the street that sells gourmet foodstuffs is a good source of referrals for your French/Danish cookware store. Talk to the owner and let her know you're there. Send her customers and the favor will be returned.

Do you have the resources?

If you are going into a service business, how about joining forces with other people in related activities? A group of women in Los Angeles have developed quite a productive arrangement that involves management consultants in compensation, affirmative action, training, placement, and audio-visual materials. One's expertise can always complement another's, and there are many times when one woman gets a lead on a job that's right down her associate's alley. Men learned this trick years ago. Now women in service businesses are learning it too.

Contacts can also help you when it comes to extra hands to help you run your business. At the beginning, you may not be able to employ anyone on a full-time basis. Wouldn't it be nice to have a friend who would be willing to work part-time as needed? There are usually friends like that around if you look for them.

Jackie Cappelli found friends like that in Peggy Dunn and Nikki Tomasello. When Jackie opened her store, The Bay Window, in Torrance, California, she was up to her shoulders in last-minute details. She wanted to open before the Christmas season but still had a great deal to do. Peggy offered to trim the windows for her and help with the layout of the store and its merchandise and Nikki tagged and hung all the garments. Now Peggy works part-time as Jackie's buyer, and Nikki works full-time in the shop.

Do you have people like that you can call on? "Mom and pop" businesses had the answer in the good old days: they enlisted the whole family. But now we're talking about "mom" businesses—and there may or may not be a pop and kids around to help out.

And kids may not always be qualified to help out. Mimi is a divorced mother with three kids who bought an existing print shop and printing press. Since it was the only "speedy" print shop in a suburb of more than 70,000 people, it was doing very well. Mimi had the monopoly on printing, but what she didn't have was a reliable pressman. She thought her teenaged kids could

The Entrepreneurial Woman

help, but she was quickly cured of that notion. She says, "Think twice about bringing your kids in to help. Habits from home carry over into the business. If they're sloppy at home, watch out!" Mimi is now reconsidering whether she wants to remain in the printing business. She found out it's really a rough business, and the demands it makes on her time and energy may be excessive at this time in her life. Mimi should have talked to another print shop owner or worked in a print shop before she bought this business. In this case more preparation was needed.

Your contacts should also include experts in law and accounting. An attorney can help you understand local laws, can help you decide whether to set up a corporation or partnership, and generally keep you out of trouble. An accountant can help set up your books, prepare a financial statement, show you how to avoid problems with the IRS, and help you use the tax laws to your advantage.

So what's the point of all this? Check out your contacts. And look before you leap! If you've got a friend like Peggy Dunn in the wings, consider yourself lucky. But, on the other hand, if all you have to rely on is your kids, maybe you'd better wait awhile. The contacts you'll need are those who'll help you, ones you can count on for information, advice, support, and even money.

MONEY

Can you ask your friends for money? Do you have enough of your own? Most new businesses need to begin with the owner's personal financial resources because few lenders give money without a credit history and a successful business track record.

Loré Caulfield had an excellent idea for a business, but to the average corporate lender, it sounded like a long shot. She wanted to manufacture silk lingerie, and she felt there was a large market for it. She knew women were earning more money,

Do you have the resources?

many were financially independent, designer clothes were selling better than ever, and she couldn't find a silk bikini for herself anywhere in Los Angeles. Loré figured there were more women like her who would pay for the luxury of silk if only they could find it. But try to sell an idea like that to the reasonably prudent male banker.

Loré's dressmaker made her some silk bikinis, she showed them to her friends, and even sold a few. She knew she was on the right track and was willing to gamble on her idea. One thing led to another, and in a matter of weeks, Loré Lingerie was born, with two dressmakers sewing and Loré designing the line from her home. She was turning out 100 silk bikinis every week and had added slips and gowns to the line when the operation began to overwhelm her. Silk, because it is so expensive, soon depleted her funds as she experimented in her home with different models. She knew that in order to keep up with the demands, she needed more help and space to conduct her business, and money to pay for the materials, help, and space. This time she looked for money to borrow. The logical place to go in the garment business is to a factor, who loans manufacturers money and takes a commission on orders or accounts receivable.

Loré borrowed from a factor, thinking that her customers would pay a markup large enough to cover her costs and allow her to stay above water and keep growing. Loré knew she had a product that was selling, but the cash flow was going to make it happen. She had to pay for her silk on order, because there is not much credit around when you're importing fabric. She had to pay her help, she had to pay overhead, she had to pay shipping. She paid, and she paid, and she paid. When was someone going to pay her? Big department stores, she found, didn't pay their bills on time, and that's the downfall of many small manufacturers. It didn't seem fair, especially after she had worked so hard!

Fortunately, Loré had joined with a number of women who were striving to make their mark in the business world. They had started a mutual support group in Los Angeles called Women in

The Entrepreneurial Woman

Business. She decided to risk asking friends for money, and five of her friends came up with enough money to float her over the rough spots. She paid her friends less interest than she paid the factors, but more than the banks would have paid them. Today, three years later, she employs twenty people in a 10,000-square-foot plant, has a fully operating manufacturing concern, and Loré Lingerie is sold in the best department stores and specialty shops throughout the world. She even has a line of credit with the bank.

HOW MUCH MONEY?—WHERE DO I GET IT?

How much money you'll need will depend on the kind of business you want to start. Many women have started businesses in their homes on a shoestring. Carolyn started hers with part of her food budget. Her hobby was covering boxes and frames with fabric. Several of her friends asked if she would make frames and mirrors to match their kids' rooms. Carolyn didn't know what to charge, but she decided she'd charge for materials plus a fair amount for the time it took her to make the frames. By keeping that money separate, she saved enough to hire a young college student to help her on an hourly, part-time basis.

The success she enjoyed with friends and acquaintances gave her the confidence to go out and sell her frames to stores. Then she hit it big. A buyer from a large hotel chain saw her frames in a specialty shop, got in touch with her, and gave her a contract to provide covered frames for thousands of its rooms. Her business has moved to her garage, she's employing four full-time workers, and last year she earned more than $60,000 in her "hobby." Now that's BIG BUSINESS! Carolyn didn't need to sit down and write a business plan before she started. She didn't even need to read books on how to start a business. The point is that she started with a minimal investment and reinvested her profits in the business to make it grow.

Do you have the resources?

Noreen St. Pierre, of St. Pierre Associates in Santa Monica, California, sells multimedia training programs to schools and industry. She needed a great deal of money to start her business, research the materials, and produce and market her products. She was able to call upon an old friend who was willing to lend her the money for a percentage of the profits. It has taken Noreen three years to build her business, but she now has the track record to get a bank loan in her own name.

What about bank loans? Well, the sad truth is that banks are not terribly interested in making loans to small businesses unless you've got excellent collateral or are an established business with a good track record. But the best friend you can have in the long run is your banker, so get to know the manager of your local bank. He or she will be able to fill you in on loan requirements and help you establish credit. Even if you have enough money initially to open your business, GET TO KNOW YOUR BANKER! You never know when you'll need more money to expand the business. The Small Business Administration's loans may also be a source of financing. Check with your local SBA office for requirements.

The SBA also offers a very good pamphlet, *Checklist for Going into Business,* to help you calculate how much money you'll need to start your business and keep it running for a period of time. It's available along with several other booklets from your local SBA office, or write the United States Small Business Administration, 1030 15th Street, N.W., Washington, D.C. 20417. It's imperative to evaluate your money needs at the beginning. It will save you a lot of surprises later.

At the same, time you should ask yourself some other money questions. How much money do you need to live on? What can you offer as collateral for a loan? Can you afford to live without a salary for a year or two? If you can't live without a salary, you will have to take into consideration family living expenses as part of your business budget. People who start businesses on a shoestring generally have some other sources of support for living expenses. Do you believe in yourself enough to take a loan on

The Entrepreneurial Woman

your life insurance, your home, or whatever other capital you have? Do you have an "angel" in your family or among your friends who's willing to lend you the money? Can you work at two jobs for a few years until you save enough money to invest in your business?

You're going to need supplies, materials, promotion, helping hands, and a place to operate your business. All this takes money or VERY GOOD FRIENDS.

If you have a good idea and you're willing to work very hard, you might be able to interest an investor in your idea. Smart investors know that most entrepreneurs will work harder for their own business than they would for anyone else. It never occurs to them that they might not know how to do something, so the chances are they'll go out and do it anyway. Their enthusiasm and lack of fear puts them one step ahead of the crowd. This attitude is contagious, and it can spread to the people you need to impress—the people with money to invest. If you're going to be an entrepreneur, you're going to have to be tenacious. Be tenacious in your quest for money. Talk to everyone you know. Maybe someone you meet will be willing to take a chance on you. You'll need to believe in yourself enough so they'll believe in you, and your attitude, more than anything else, may be the deciding factor in getting someone to take a gamble.

While we're on the subject of money, here's a final thought for you. It's called "risking the family jewels."

If your husband had a sensational idea for a business, is there any question you would mortgage the home or sell the stock to raise the money? Probably not. But too many women have the attitude that they don't have the right to risk the family money; it's for the husband to decide. It's a question of self-esteem, partnership, sharing. It comes down to the question: ARE YOU WORTH IT? Think about it—I'll bet you are!

After reading this chapter, you may feel as though your head is spinning. You don't know where to begin? How do you know

Do you have the resources?

who will be a resource for you and who won't? To review all you've read, take a few moments to go over the checklists on the following pages. It will help you to get organized. There are no right answers to these checklists. They are merely an inventory of your resources. They will help you identify what you have and what you might need.

$$

CHECKLIST FOR RESOURCES

Resource #1. YOU!

Check the personality traits you think you have.

____Chutzpah

____Intelligence

____Tenacity

____Patience

____Organization

____Optimism

____Enthusiasm

____High need for achievement

____Ability to set goals

____Ability to solve problems

____Independent

____Self-confident

____Energetic

____Willing to take calculated risks

____Willing to take responsibility for self

____Love to win

Resource #2. YOU AND YOUR EXPERIENCE

Check the experience you have, even if it's from running a home or volunteer work.

____Budgeting
____Organizing
____Delegating
____Public Relations
____Advertising
____Planning
____Directing
____Coordinating
____Evaluating
____Hiring and firing
____Goal setting

____Presenting
____Selling
____Counseling
____Problem solving
____Raising money
____Researching
____Buying
____Shipping/delivery
____Communicating
____Keeping books

Resource #3. YOU AND COMMITMENT

How much time can you give to your business?
_____

What priorities do you have in your life now?
_____
_____
_____

How much of your time will these priorities take?
_____

Can any of these be put aside for a year or two while you start your business?_____Which ones?
_____
_____

Do you have the resources?

Now that you've answered the above questions, how many hours per week will you devote to your business? _____

Resource #4. YOU AND YOUR CONTACTS

What kind do you have and what kind do you need?

_____

_____

Who are the first people you're going to talk to about your business?

_____

_____

_____

Who do you know who can help you in setting up your business?

- _____An attorney?
- _____An accountant?
- _____A banker?
- _____A friend (perhaps to cover for you when the kids are sick)?
- _____Someone who's in the same type of business?
- _____A member of your family?

What professional business groups can you go to for the information you need.

_____

_____

_____

_____

Resource #5. YOU AND MONEY

Check the statements that are true.

_____ I know how much money I have of my own to put into a business.

_____ I know how much money is necessary to get my business started.

_____ I know how much credit I can get from suppliers.

_____ I know where I can borrow the rest of the money I need to start.

_____ I know how much money I need to live on.

_____ I've estimated how much money I can expect to earn from my business the first year.

_____ I have a lawyer, banker, and accountant I can talk with.

_____ I can "risk the family jewels" because I'm worth it.

_____ I have a good idea of what I'll have to pay employees, both in salary and benefits.

_____ I've researched the tax implications of my business.

_____ I've researched insurance needs and costs.

_____ I'm willing to spend money to make money.

If you've checked all the above points, you've done your homework. If you've missed a few, you might have some more preparing to do.

$$

$$$$$$$$ 3 $$$$$$$$
What kind of business?

"Heads, I open a boutique, tails, I go into real estate."

How many people do you know who've said, "I want to go into business for myself, but I don't know what I want to do"? The choices are mind-boggling. If the only thing you are sure of is that you want to be your own boss and make lots of money, that's OK. That's where it usually starts.

You may already have an idea for a product or service, but you still have second thoughts: "Is this the idea? Is there a better one?" Even if you have already started your business, you may sometimes feel there is something else you should be doing. You may still not be sure if you should open a store, manufacture a product, or sell a service.

Perhaps you should buy an existing business or invest in some kind of franchise or just find a partner with an idea?

If these thoughts run through your mind, you are not so different from other women. I've talked with 250 women representing 350 businesses, and all felt the same way at one time.

This chapter will help you clarify your thinking, help you come up with an idea based on your experience and needs, and give you examples of how other women have zeroed in on their business ideas. It won't tell you what to do, because you're the only one who can decide that.

By now you should have a pretty good idea of who you are as a latent entrepreneur and as your own best resource. What conclusions can you make about your own uniqueness? Do you

The Entrepreneurial Woman

prefer to work with people or by yourself? Do you like to gather information and use it yourself, or do you like to put things together for other people to use? Do you work best with data, people, or things? Are you outgoing, enthusiastic, energetic, or are you somewhat reserved and shy? Your likes and dislikes and personality will influence the type of business you run.

CAREER-SEARCH TECHNIQUES THAT WORK

John L. Holland, who has done an enormous amount of research and work in career planning, states that basically all work falls into six interest and ability clusters or environments. These are the Realistic, Investigative, Artistic, Social, Enterprising, and Conventional. These work environments are more thoroughly discussed in his book, *Making Vocational Choices: A Theory of Careers* (Prentice-Hall, 1973).

There are thousands of job titles that fall within these clusters, and jobs overlap into several environments. But to get an idea of what these descriptions mean as they relate to your world of work, read on. As you're reading, think about which areas your interest and abilities coincide with.

The Realistic involves mechanical abilities and interests. Think of Josephine the Lady Plumber; she's working in a realistic field. So is a woman I talked with who owns a gas station. She had spent a lot of time pinch-hitting in her husband's service station and, a few years ago, decided to buy her own. She loves the mechanics of cars, being outside, and kibitzing with the customers. She doesn't mind getting her hands greasy or crawling under a car on a scooter board. When I asked her about her work, she said, "I wish I had done this years ago. My husband let me work only part-time when he needed an extra hand in his station, and now, he has his station, I have mine, and I can call my own shots."

What kind of business?

The Investigative is just what it implies. It involves problem solving, and includes engineering, computers, and other scientific fields. One of the most interesting entrepreneurial women I've met is Susan Herman. She worked for many years as a medical technologist in Pennsylvania but decided five years ago to open her own lab. She now employs eight assistants and has contracts from many doctors to do their lab work.

The Artistic includes theater, writing, crafts, interior design, fabric design, fashion design, photography, painting, ceramics, sculpture, needlework, quilting, etc. No doubt you have seen lots of hobby and craft ideas grow into successful businesses. Pat Esler runs an art gallery in New Mexico, specializing in native American arts. She had collected Indian pottery and baskets from the time she was a youngster, and when she saw how popular this type of art was becoming, she recognized the opportunity to open her gallery. Her knowledge of this art form and her contacts with the artists on the reservations gave her the resources to begin.

Social Environments involve the helping and service professions, such as teaching, counseling, and home economics. You'll find many women-owned businesses that have been established in this area. Think of the private schools, exercise classes, beauty shops, dance studios, career development and counseling centers, and weight reduction programs that have been started by women and built into large businesses. Certainly, Jean Nidetch's Weight Watchers International, Inc., qualifies.

The Enterprising area involves selling and management. By definition it is a key part of all entrpreneurial ventures, including yours. It covers most independent store owners and manufacturers and those corporate people such as buyers, merchandisers, account executives, and others who sell ideas, products, or services for the corporation. Even if you consider yourself an artistic or realistic entrepreneur, you're going to need to feel

The Entrepreneurial Woman

comfortable with the enterprising aspect of the world of work. Freelance writers and artists either have to be enterprising or get agents to sell their work and get assignments. Peggy Leach Connolly turned her corporate experience of marketing and business systems into an entrepreneurial venture. Her business, WP Temps, places word-processing temporaries in major companies in Los Angeles.

The Conventional involves clerical and administrative work. It includes the office skills of record keeping, typing, and bookkeeping. If you see this administrative field as something you enjoy, you might, like Ruth Oreck, think of starting a secretarial service. Ruth's business, Oreck Association Management, is unique in that it specializes in administration for several business and professional organizations in Los Angeles. Her company provides management services and acts as headquarters for activities of these groups by handling their telephone inquiries, monthly mailings, newsletters, and statements. Ruth's firm also works with the boards of directors to implement policies, set up and administer meetings and conferences, develop membership, budgets, and awards.

Most people come up with a combination of two or three of these fields of interest when they do career investigation exercises. If you want to try a more structured approach to finding where you lean, check out Holland's book. In it you'll find "The Self-directed Search," a vocational inventory. It is self-scoring, and self-administered. You'll come up with a code of three letters representing your strengths in the six skill and interest clusters outlined above. Once you come up with your code, you can use Holland's book to find hundreds of job titles consistent with your skills and interests. Many of these can be turned into independent business ventures.

To carry this exercise one step farther, go to the library with your code in hand and look through the *Dictionary of Occupational Titles* (DOT). Holland's code translates into the DOT

What kind of business?

codes. This book, published by the U.S. Department of Labor, has thousands of job titles and descriptions of the skills necessary to perform the work. It's all explained in great detail in Holland's book, so if you're really floundering, it could be one of the best ways to help you pinpoint a field.

There are other fine career-development resources you can explore to help you get your own private answer to this all-important question. There are courses at local schools, career counselors, and books. Many of these will suggest a number of exercises such as the ones that follow. Take the time to do them. They'll help you see if you're going in the right direction. But you'll still have to put on your track shoes to do the legwork to find the business that suits you.

Career planning, to be effective, involves the past as well as the present and future. You build on previous experience, and because you've had the chance in previous chapters to see what drives you, what your personality traits are, let's start there.

Take a look at your past . . . what did you do? Let's look at the years when you were between fifteen and twenty.

____What were your hobbies?

____How did you do in school?

____What did you excel in?

____What did you enjoy?

____Did you have a job? If so, doing what?

____What extracurricular activities did you take part in?

____What about sports? Were you involved?

____What environment did you enjoy best?

____Inside? Outside?

____With people? Alone?

____In the city? Country?

The Entrepreneurial Woman

Get some paper and a pencil and answer these questions with as much detail as you can remember about yourself during those five years. Think in terms of home, school, work, hobbies, friends, and extracurricular activities. When you're finished with this chapter in your life (you will take your time and write several pages, won't you?), look at these pages and on another piece of paper make separate columns for the things you wrote down. Your columns should look like this:

WHAT I DID	WHERE I DID IT	WHAT I LIKED ABOUT IT	WHAT I DIDN'T LIKE

Now, look at these columns and find the things you loved doing and want to keep on doing and write them down on another piece of paper. Also make a list of things you don't want to do any more.

Of the things you loved, why did you enjoy them? Was it because of the people, challenge, environment, or things you were involved with? Can you make any inferences yet about what you liked and enjoyed about your past? Write them down.

Do this exercise again for the years between twenty and twenty-five. Do you see any differences emerging? Write them down. Keep doing this exercise for five-year periods in your life. Do any patterns come up? This is one way to get in touch with what you enjoy doing, what you've done, what you've learned, and what you want to keep doing.

Look over these pages. Were you a self-starter? Did you determine what needed to be done and then do it? Were you able

What kind of business?

to motivate yourself to work and thus experience doing "your thing"? If you were a self-starter, you were able to carry out most of your activities without a lot of outside direction or instruction or pats on the back. Were you comfortable with responsibility? Did you seek it out, just accept it, or avoid it altogether?

Were you a leader? Did you motivate others to work or to get involved? Were you able to give instructions and supervise activities of those involved with you? One woman I know went through this self-investigation process and was amazed to rediscover that she had started several clubs as a teenager and had been the instigator of several school activities. She recognized her supervisory skills and leadership ability as part of this process. She also recognized that she had carried over these attributes into her adult life by organizing neighborhood and school-related committees for the benefit of her community. She's putting those talents to work now as a consultant for several organizations specializing in charitable fund-raising.

Were you an instigator? Most entrepreneurs are. Did you plant the seeds in other people's heads and then let them carry out your ideas? Were you happy in the background, just as long as you could see someone else doing what you thought needed to be done? Were you the kid in the student council who had the courage to confront the administration of the school with suggested curriculum changes? Did you like to formulate policies and see them carried out? Were you persuasive?

Gloria Brown is an instigator. If you ask her what she does, she'll say she runs a hospital gift shop. But there's more to her story than that. Gloria is the wife of a doctor in a midwestern city. She knew she wanted a business of her own, but she also knew she didn't want to give her money to the government, because she and her husband were already in a high tax bracket.

She opened a gift shop to benefit the hospital, sell quality merchandise, and allow her the opportunity to manage a business and see the profits grow. The shop was an outlet for her

The Entrepreneurial Woman

entrepreneurial energies. While Gloria doesn't take a salary from the business, she does take out-of-town buying trips, a *bona fide* business expense. She's also built a business with volunteer help. The hospital auxiliary members work in the gift shop for their "hours," and some of them have even advanced to the rank of buyers and merchandise managers.

A California woman, Merrilee Goldman, tells a similar story. Her gift shop, The Rainbow, supports a pediatric oncology wing at Cedars Sinai Hospital in Los Angeles. The Rainbow also sells some of its handcraft items nationally. I remember seeing its cookbook in a department store in Cincinnati.

Both Merrilee Goldman and Gloria Brown are instigators. Their ideas have grown into big businesses even though they are not in it for personal profit. They are both entrepreneurs of no less merit than Henry Ford.

Did you teach, advise, or counsel others? Were you a guide for others in problem solving? Susan had been a head counselor in a girls' camp for two summers during her college years and has been involved with the Girl Scouts and Y-Teens as a volunteer. She'd completely overlooked those experiences when she took stock of herself and looked into business possibilities. She's still in the process of deciding on how best to put these interests and skills to work in a business, but so far, she's come up with the following ideas: opening a recreation center for teenagers in her community; starting a sports camp for girls, using the facilities of a local private school; and starting a travel program for teenagers, hiring teachers to be guides, organizing and selling the tours through the local private schools. All three of these business ideas interest her, and she's investigating the market potential for each, calculating the finances, and talking to everyone she can about working with teenagers. She's raised three of her own, so she has a pretty good idea of what's in store.

All of this thinking and writing can take you several days if you give it the thought and time it deserves. Finding out about your own internal needs and external likes and dislikes is THE

What kind of business?

BASIC FIRST STEP IN CAREER MAKING. Finding a job or the right business is a full-time job!

Now, take a look at your future. Daydream a little bit. What do you want for a lifestyle? What do you need? How much money? What about your family? What about YOU?

WHAT ABOUT YOUR NEEDS?

Your financial and geographic needs will definitely influence your choice of business. Ask yourself these questions "Is it important for me to maintain my current standard of living?" "What about my family, are they willing to make sacrifices for my business success?"

Pat Robertson changed her life dramatically so she could afford to open her business. She's the divorced mother of two boys and had spent fifteen years working for others. Her experience was in public relations, and she wanted to be her own boss. But in order to finance this venture, she had to sell her house. Her children supported her in her belief that it was a worthwhile risk.

Write down a list of all the things you value about your present lifestyle. What would you have to give up or change in order to give the time and commitment to a business? What things do you want to be a part of your future lifestyle that aren't on the present list? Will opening your own business help you to get those things—or at least some of them?

Sheila O'Brien's future list, when she started her travel agency, included the need to set down roots in Los Angeles. She's English, had worked for Pan American, and was based in Los Angeles. The chance of Pan Am transferring her was always real. By starting her travel agency and leaving the airline, she gained the roots and the base she wanted.

If you've gone through the preceding steps, you should know what you'd like to do and what you'd like to avoid. If it looks like too much trouble and takes too much energy to

The Entrepreneurial Woman

complete, maybe you won't or don't have the energy to start a business. If that seems to be the case, maybe the time isn't right for you or maybe you're still waiting for the great idea to come along. Sometimes the opportunity presents itself . . . but it STILL MUST BE YOU who takes advantage of it!

Julie Lopp Karno was a new divorcee with two young children. Her needs were immense. She knew she'd have to support her kids, but she didn't know how. At the time of her divorce, she'd been working part-time as a teacher, but she HATED teaching! She'd worked in advertising and public relations before her marriage, and she'd dabbled in the theater and in business. Her father was a candy maker in Wisconsin, where she grew up, so she'd learned a little bit about that business. But the thought of going into her own business hadn't yet occurred to Julie. She only knew she'd have to come up with a way to make money fast. She felt that she could always go back to teaching as a last resort, but that left her cold. Julie was biding time in Los Angeles, taking a few classes in business administration when opportunity came knocking.

Her uncle in Reno was after her Dad to open a candy shop in Nevada. For Dad it was the wrong time—and the wrong town. But for Julie it was an idea worth investigating. The next steps were easy. As she tells it, the most important decision was LOCATION, LOCATION, AND LOCATION! Within a week, she was off to Virginia City to talk to the people, to get a feeling for them, for the area, and for the business traffic in different locations. Virginia City is a tourist town, and tourist traffic was going to be very important to Julie's business.

She also knew she'd need some special twist to make her business a winner. Her grandmother, a woman Julie admired, had just died. She had been an active, impressive lady and an independent businesswoman, and so the idea was born. "Grandma's Fudge"! That name lent itself to an early American feeling and a quality, homemade product. Julie's theatrical background

What kind of business?

proved helpful in expressing that theme throughout the store. She used blue and white gingham, copper pots, costumes for the employees, and the ambience of an early settler's kitchen. You would have thought you had walked into the nineteenth century by the time Julie was finished with her "set."

Television's "Bonanza" series helped put Virginia City on the map. It was as close to a populated ghost town as you could find in the West, and Julie's decor fit right in with the tourists' expectations. The whole thing tied together when Julie opened for business in the summer of 1971. A few years later, she opened her second store in Palm Springs, California, another vacation spot. The irony of it all hit Julie that first night as she rang up the cash register in the Virginia City store: "I thought, here I am again, I've traveled all over the world, had all sorts of experiences, and here I am, right back where I started as a twelve-year-old in Daddy's candy store!"

Sounds like it all came together for Julie, doesn't it? But from her story, we can draw the conclusion that present needs and past experiences do play an important part in business selection for entrepreneurial women.

Julie also sounds like the classic entrepreneur. She was displaced, divorced . . . remember? She had the role models . . . father and grandmother. She was willing to take the risk of moving to a new town. She was independent, and she had the resources. Her father, who'd been in the candy business for years, was a contact, a source of information and references for her. Suppliers were willing to give her credit on his word, the recipe for the fudge came from his resources, the technical "how to" also came from him. But it was Julie's own knowledge of public relations, the people skills she had learned as a teacher, the knowledge of costuming and decor she'd picked up from her theater experience, and her personality and determination that helped carry the whole thing off!

I asked Julie how she got through that first year in a strange town with two babies, a new business, and no friends to help. She

The Entrepreneurial Woman

told me three things kept her going. First, fear . . . fear of starving and losing what she had started. Second, a key employee: she'd hired a young high school kid to help her make the fudge and run the store. And third, a kooky, charming boyfriend who kept her laughing, helped her with the maintenance chores, and gave her encouragement as she went along. He was food for her soul; he kept her spirits high and gave her moral support. She never really gave failure a chance.

Julie also gives the other men she knows a lot of credit for helping her develop her business expertise. Today she's got the financial security she started out to achieve, and she's also got the knowledge that she's a highly qualified businessperson. The children are older now, and Julie wants to spend some more time with them. She's president of Grandma's Enterprises and has developed a franchise package for Grandma's Fudge stores. Her stores are successful, she's hired and trained competent people, and she's looking ahead to a career spin-off for herself. She'll be a consultant to Grandma's Fudge shops across the country. Her success has allowed her the freedom to take time off, to be with her children, and to have some fun.

There's a moral in this story, of course. It's been said before, and it will be said again in this book. That is, know yourself, and go after what you want!

PARTNERS, FRANCHISES, AND COMMUNITY RESOURCES

What if you know you've got organizational skill, "stick-to-it-iveness," but still no idea? What about finding a partner with an idea? Or, what if the opposite is true? You've got the idea but need someone with resources to turn your idea into a business. If you're the one with the idea but no wherewithal to carry it out, consider Peggy's story.

Peggy dreamed up an idea for a toy. It was a game that she

What kind of business?

thought would have broad appeal to children. She investigated the possibility of making and selling it herself, but the whole manufacturing-marketing process scared her. She sold her idea to a major toy company, but the company never produced the toy, so she never realized any royalties from it.

Looking back on that venture today, she recognizes she could have gone another way. This is what she says: "I could have gotten my idea patented, found a good marketing person, cut him or her into the deal on a partnership basis, and then let the marketing person sell the idea to a manufacturer with some sales guarantees. The marketing person would have developed the strategy to interest a major manufacturer in going ahead with the project." Instead, Peggy allowed her lack of experience and investigation to stand in the way of developing more ideas for the toy industry.

A partner should be someone who can add a resource you don't have. That resource can be money, a source of supplies, or a talent you don't have.

Sharon's partnership was born because an old college friend, Maryanne, was moving to the Philippines. Sharon saw this as a great opportunity to go into the import business, bringing in fabrics and baskets for the gift trade. Sharon knew a lot about design and fashion and had a great knack for choosing "in" things. She also had terrific sales ability and wasn't afraid to try a new venture. Maryanne, on the other hand, hadn't given much thought to business, although Sharon's enthusiasm got to her.

Before Maryanne left for the Philippines, she and Sharon spent a great deal of time comparison shopping. They went to a gift show, to specialty shops, fabric houses, and basket shops. It was an educational process for both of them. It gave Sharon the chance to show Maryanne the kinds of things she should look for in the Philippines, what they'd be able to sell them for, and what they could create a market for.

When Maryanne got to the Philippines, she began looking

The Entrepreneurial Woman

for unique items to export. In the meantime, Sharon was learning all there was to learn about importing. She researched the laws, talking to the experts, and set up the business as a legal corporation. Maryanne finally located some terrific gift possibilities and sent the samples to Sharon, who sold the line to a major department-store chain. They were on their way! After the first orders were delivered and reorders came in, they knew they had a winner. Then a typhoon hit the islands. The suppliers were unable to produce the goods, headache number one in the importing business. Sharon really learned a lot about importing that year. She found out that you can't count on anything in that business and that a lot of problems come from factors completely beyond one's control.

When I asked her what were the best parts about having a partner, she said, "A partner can give you the kick in the pants you occasionally need. She can share the frustrations, give you the incentive to keep plugging, help keep your confidence up." I asked her, "Would you have a partner again?" She said, "No, it gets too complicated." Maryanne is now going through a divorce, and the corporation has to be closed out for tax and settlement purposes. But Sharon hasn't given up, and her experiences have helped her in setting up her new business venture.

Judy Chasalow agrees that a partner can be the one to keep you going. She and her partner started an interior design business a year ago. They find that they complement and motivate each other. Neither feels she'd be as successful on her own. It's hard to let your partner down, since GUILT is an excellent motivator for some people. Even though Judy and her partner had thought about going into the interior design business at various times, both agree they never would have taken the step alone.

What about buying into an existing business as a partner? Is this something you're willing to consider? You need to ask the same questions. Is it the kind of business I want to be in? Does it fit in with who I am? Then you'll need to check out the business

What kind of business?

itself. Why is this person selling a part of the business? Has she expanded too fast? Does she need your money to stay in business? What is the state of the business? The time to get a good financial reading of the business is before you commit yourself to a partnership. The same advice holds true if you're buying an existing business outright.

Do you know of the tremendous resources in your community for locating an existing business that's up for sale? Are you aware there are people who buy and sell businesses? They are called business brokers and you can find them in the yellow pages of your local phone book. If you live in a big city, you might be amazed to find two or three columns of business brokers in the book. Business brokers have listings on existing businesses and operate pretty much the same as real estate brokers. They'll give you the names of businesses for sale, but you won't get escorted to the site. If you buy a business through a broker lead, it won't cost you anything beyond the purchase price. The seller pays the commission. Generally, to use the services of business brokers, you'll need a $15,000 to $20,000 minimum investment.

Newspapers in general and *The Wall Street Journal* in particular also list business opportunities. They run the gamut from partnerships to franchises. You'll find everything from coffee and beauty shops to car and airplane washes, dry cleaners, laundromats, junkyards, lumberyards, and worm farms. These columns make fascinating reading and could help you find your fortune.

What about franchises? What does a franchise offer that an existing business doesn't? The right franchise offers you a proven better chance for success than if you had to start from scratch, but the number of flaky franchises available should make you approach the field with your eyes wide open.

Basically a franchise is a license that allows you to sell, make, or distribute a product or service in a particular area under an established system or marketing plan. When you buy a franchise, you buy a brand name, a proven record, and the benefits of someone else's learning. Generally, you'll get some help along with your purchase. You might get advertising and promotion, site selection, financing assistance, special prices on equipment and supplies, and continuing counseling.

A franchiser may charge you a royalty on sales, require you to contribute to an advertising fund, and buy your supplies through its sources. Further, you may have to agree to adhere to the franchiser's standards and practices and open your operation to its inspection. Franchising has so many problems that you should approach this area of entrepreneurship with the help of someone who really knows this type of business. Worthwhile reading on franchising is available from:

1. The International Franchise Association, 7315 Wisconsin Avenue, Washington, D.C. 20014 (*Investigate Before Investing*).
2. The Bank of America, Department 3120, P.O. Box 3700, San Francisco, California 94137 (*The Small Business Reporter*, special issue on franchising, cost: $1).
3. Sylvia Porter's *Money Book*, published by Doubleday and Company.

Again, if you decide you want to go the franchise route, ask yourself whether it fits in with who you are. How does it fit in with your needs for the future?

Now that you've read this chapter and gone through the career-planning exercises, you are probably very close to deciding on your chosen field. If you're still not 100 percent sure, here's an idea for you: test market! That's right, try it, see if you like it. If you have decided to open a gift shop, go to work in one for a short while. Want to start a counseling business? Hook on with a counselor for a few months. You'll not only gain invaluable experience in your chosen field, but you will also learn if it's

What kind of business?

the field for you at a very small risk.

So many businesses fail because the owners have a poor sense of direction, no stated goals, or simply go into the business because it seems like a good idea at the time. They operate like the fanatics who say, "We've lost sight of our goal, but we have redoubled our efforts!"

The time to redouble your efforts is now, before you have invested a lot of time and energy in a given field. Make sure that your chosen field takes advantage of the tremendous experience you have rediscovered, that it relates to your skill and ability clusters, that it recognizes the advantages and disadvantages of partnerships, franchises, or existing businesses as they relate to you and only you.

$$$$$$$$ 4 $$$$$$$$
Self-confidence

No one can make you feel inferior without your consent.
—*Eleanor Roosevelt*

To build your self-confidence, have you been Rolfed, ESTed, learned mind control, had a peak experience through Gestalt therapy, or a close encounter with a maharishi? Do you know if you can "Increase Your Inner Energy," move into an "Alpha State," "Take Charge of Your Life," or "Be Your Own Best Friend"? To enhance your self-esteem, are you "Winning Through Intimidation"? Have you gone through the journey of self-discovery only to discover you have too many "Erroneous Zones" to conquer? Do you come away from these sessions of self-exploration finding it impossible to believe that "Any Woman Can"?

Welcome to the club!

There is a great deal of self-doubt in our society. We are taught to be modest to the point of self-denigration, to defer to others, to believe that success in any endeavor is extremely difficult. Even the attempts to instruct us in the art of self-help don't help much.

"Every time I read a self-help book, I'm convinced I've got so far to go that I can't even start," said Carla, a thirty-five-year-old lab technician in one of my UCLA Extension seminars. "I do what the book says for a while, I don't see any change, so I feel even lousier about myself."

Another woman named Jane chimed in, "Even if I start to change, I get so much static from my family, it makes me feel

The Entrepreneurial Woman

worse. I get the feeling they don't want me to change. They want their chief cook and bottle-washer cooking and washing bottles."

Suddenly all the women in the group were talking at once. Someone had hit a sensitive nerve. People desperately want help and actively seek it, but don't always get the support needed to bring about the necessary changes.

We may sometimes feel as though we're in a crisis, and don't possess the nerve or the energy to deal with it. Not dealing with this negative self-image decreases our sense of self-worth and keeps us locked in a rut, further depressing our self-image. We become immobilized. Self-defeating behavior gets in our way.

So what can be done to break this cycle?

You need self-confidence and a positive outlook to be fulfilled, but the advice on how to do this is overwhelming, confusing, and often contradictory. Don't give up yet! In this chapter we'll look at the problem in more personal terms, relate it to the needs of the female entrepreneur, and attempt to set your mind at ease. And in the chapters that follow, we'll outline steps that others have found helpful in gaining confidence.

Does an entrepreneur need self-confidence? Only about as much as a fish needs water!

As an entrepreneur, your self-confidence can make up for deficiencies in many other areas. It can help you overcome the doubts of friends, family creditors, customers, bankers, and even yourself. If you believe in what you are doing, you can make others believe through an unshakable self-confidence.

You will need self-confidence daily to run your business successfully:

—— to demand deliveries and services when you need them, not when *they* want to supply them;

—— to obtain work from your own suppliers and employees that is up to your high standards;

—— to charge your customers what you honestly feel they should pay for your efforts;

Self-confidence

——to say "No" to people who waste your time or drain your resources;

——to create the kind of environment that makes customers want to do business with you.

You will face such problems every day. Since the buck starts and stops with you, you're going to have to take charge, and for that you'll need a sense of self-worth that allows you to act. If you're self-confident, you'll find it easier to deal with customers and suppliers who give you a hard time. You won't have to worry about whether or not they like you—you'll just worry about what's best for the business. You'll have the ability to live your own life, set your own goals, and make the best use of your abilities.

So, how do all these accomplished women you read about get this self-confidence?

How can you ever get your own?

You may ask because you are not entirely sure of yourself. Well, the truth is that no one is ever entirely sure of herself (or *him*self either)! I've talked with hundreds of businessmen and businesswomen over these past five years about their feelings of self-confidence. They all confess to days and even weeks when they are consumed with self-doubt. No matter how decisively they behave on the job, there are times when they need reassurance, a sign, a stroke to say that they are OK. There are days when corporate vice-presidents feel like staying home, safe and warm, under the covers. Ultimately, they do regain that self-confidence and go on with the job at hand.

The point is that you can create, control, and maintain your self-confidence if you understand the factors that influence how you feel about yourself.

You can take charge of your own self-confidence even if the world conspires against you, even if you are underutilized in your current job, isolated in your suburban dream castle, bored to tears with the way you spend your days. Self-confidence flows

The Entrepreneurial Woman

from positive experiences. Build yourself a series of positive experiences. Start today by treating yourself well and trusting yourself. BE GOOD TO YOURSELF!

"If *you* don't love yourself, who will?" Remember those words from your childhood? Or were you the one who heard only "love your neighbor" or "turn the other cheek"? Many of us are so concerned about loving our neighbors and giving to others that we forget ourselves. You can choose to give yourself the emotionally fulfilling love you need. You can buy yourself presents. You can choose to stop denying yourself. Self-confident people treat themselves well. They do things they enjoy, thereby reinforcing their feelings of self-worth.

A woman I knew in St. Louis was wrestling with a mid-life crisis. Self-defeating behavior kept getting in her way. She had developed a list of "shoulds" that went like this:

"I should be concerned with who my children's friends are."

"I should make sure my children are neat and clean."

"I should be sure the children dress well for school."

"I should make sure the children get good grades."

"I should entertain my husband's business associates."

"I should do volunteer work at the children's school."

"I should have an immaculate house."

"I should cook good, nourishing meals."

"I should keep myself in good shape."

"I should keep up on the latest current events and books."

"I should take a few courses at the local college."

"I should visit my mom and dad twice a week."

"I should call and write my aunts and uncles."

"I should write my mother-in-law."

"I should make sure the children visit their grandparents."

Self-confidence

And so on, until she couldn't keep track of all her "shoulds."

Does this list sound all-too-familiar to you? Are "shoulds" and "musts" immobilizing you and getting in the way of real self-actualization? Are you too wound up with the needs and demands of others to pay attention to yourself? If there's no time left for you, you might indeed feel bogged down and "less than."

For my friend in St. Louis, the first step was to go over her list of "shoulds" and decide which ones she wanted to change. She knew she wanted to change her life, treat herself better, but she didn't have the self-confidence necessary to begin the process. Only by changing some of the "shoulds" was she able to find the time to develop her strengths, try new behavior, and build self-confidence around successful experiences. Examining the "shoulds" in your life can be a step for you, too.

In Chapter One, inner and external controls were discussed as factors in entrepreneurial success. As children, many of us were extremely controlled by "shoulds." Some of these rules and "shoulds" have been carried over to our present lives. They've allowed us to "fit in" without rocking the boat. These "shoulds" made us into "good little girls," "nice young ladies," "proper women,"—but lousy entrepreneurs because being an entrepreneur requires a type of misfit behavior. It's a risk to give up the valued opinions of others as you move out on your own. It's much easier to blame your parents, your astrologer, or your psychologist than it is to take responsibility for yourself. Well, to build your self-confidence you MUST begin by taking responsibility for yourself, and by developing your own inner center of control.

TAKING CONTROL BY TRUSTING YOURSELF

I remember an experience from music appreciation class at college. The only way to get the A I wanted was to learn how to

The Entrepreneurial Woman

play Bach's Fugue in G. Now, mind you, I'd never played the piano and I thought of myself as totally uncoordinated. Using two hands to play the piano was complicated enough, but a fugue demanded total concentration and skill in addition to coordination. I made up my mind. I decided to risk it. Now my goal was set. And do you know what happened? With practice and determination, I did it!

Instead of blaming my teacher for my inability to get an A in his class, I chose to trust myself. I made *the circumstance work for me* instead of blaming the circumstance. This experience has been repeated many times in my life. Even though I once thought I'd lost that college girl, when I need her I can resurrect her.

Is there a similar story in your past? Can you create situations today that will be successful because you trust yourself? Trust yourself with the family budget, planning your next vacation, taking one by yourself. What about taking a job? Success in a job can give you the self-trust to start out on your own.

Part of becoming a successful entrepreneur *is* trusting yourself and your decisions despite what the experts might say. This again shows an inner sense of control. You have strong feelings and good instincts, but the experts may not always see things your way. It's terribly easy, but an evasion of responsibility nonetheless, to agree blindly with the experts. Don't be afraid to get another opinion or even go against expert advice. It's *your* bottom line. Listen well, but make the ultimate decision yourself.

Susan tells just such a story about questioning the experts. Her doctor had recommended a D and C. She'd just seen the movie *Coma* and so she wasn't terribly enthusiastic about having even "minor" surgery. Fortunately, she had a woman friend who was also a gynecologist. She called the friend, told her the symptoms and her fears, and asked for her opinion. Susan's friend didn't laugh at her fantasies of terminal endometriosis, or grapefruit-sized tumors, but invited her to come in for an examination. All the things Susan had been thinking when she visited her first doctor, but had avoided asking for fear of ridicule, came out and

Self-confidence

were discussed. Susan's friend found the problem, a small polyp, which she removed in the office. There was no need for the operation because Susan had put herself in charge.

She felt a heightened sense of self-esteem after that experience, and it carried over into her business decision making. Her accountant had given her some tax advice she didn't quite understand. But she figured, why bother, Audrey must know what she's doing, she's the accountant! Susan decided after her medical experience that she wanted to "bother." So she called Audrey, asked about the tax advice, and got a clear answer, which influenced her decisions on how to expand her business. Without questioning Audrey about "Decision A" she never would have had the input for a better "Decision B."

P-I-E-S

Some of the biggest hurdles that entrepreneurial women have to overcome are imposed by the traditions of our society. There are very few laurels for the woman who starts a successful computer-programming venture, but the woman who creates a recipe for a tasty apple-crunch pie can win a Pillsbury baking contest and see herself in magazines and on television. It's those old "shoulds" again! Women *should* make good apple-crunch pie, whereas men *should* start the businesses.

These none-too-subtle messages can drain your self-confidence. Why go through the trauma of starting a business if the only recognition you'll get is from the tax collector? Why not create the ultimate fudge-nut brownie pie?

Pies can have a place in your scheme as an entrepreneur if you will look at P-I-E-S in a new light. Look at P-I-E-S as the recipe ingredients of your new-found self-confidence. Your self-confidence is made up of how you think of yourself in four areas: Physical, Intellectual, Emotional, and Social. Let's look at your self-confidence now in terms of these key ingredients.

YOUR PHYSICAL SELF-IMAGE

Start with a good look in the mirror and ask, "Mirror, mirror, on the wall, who is this person, after all?" What do you see? Someone who needs a little uplifting (not uplift, upli*fting*!)? A little confidence building? Does your appearance get you down? Are you too fat, too thin, too old, too tall, too small? How is the physical part of your self-image? Move through the following checklist quickly to see what conclusions you draw.

$$

CHECKLIST FOR PHYSICAL SELF-IMAGE

Check the statement(s) which apply to you:

_____I'm in great physical shape.

_____I'm too fat.

_____I'm too thin.

_____I like the way I look.

_____I have lots of energy for the things I want to do.

_____I feel bogged down.

_____Physically, I'm a klutz.

_____I'm a good athlete.

_____I exercise regularly.

_____I have a tendency to physical illness.

_____I get a lot of headaches.

_____These old bones of mine give me trouble.

$$

Are you feeling negative or positive about your physical self-image? What do your answers to the above questions indicate?

Self-confidence

Most women I've talked with have negative feelings about their bodies. For so many years they've heard "Stand up straight!" "Eat your dinner, you're too skinny!" "Hold in your stomach!" "Don't eat that, you'll get pimples!" "Where did that pimple come from?" "You need a little bit of makeup, you look too pale." "Your boobs are too big." "Hey, Flatsie, are you a boy or a girl?"

These childhood messages are carried over into adulthood as we're bombarded daily with commercials extolling the virtues of a flat stomach, pert breasts and flowing blond *(never grey)* hair. So who can blame us for hating the bodies we live in? Well, let me tell you, the body you live in *is* you! And you'll have to take the responsibility for whether or not you want to continue hating YOU!

I attended a women's workshop in which we were instructed to think about our bodies. The women in our group explored their feelings about their bodies and how they were working to change those feelings. One woman said, "I used to buy youth-oriented things, but now, Rubens is my man . . . and I'm falling in love with the concept of being a lush, beautiful Rubens type. I can even look at myself nude in the mirror and visualize myself in the velvet and chiffon with which Rubens adorned his women." She knew she'd never be a slight, skinny young thing again, and she was working toward total acceptance of herself.

In that workshop we did an exercise that helped us focus on what we liked and disliked about our bodies.

First, we are told, "Close your eyes, imagine yourself as you look now. Look at yourself, what do you see? Look at the hair, do you like it? What do you like about it—is it the color, the texture, the length, the style? If you don't like it, can you change it, or can you change your feelings about it?"

Next, the leader asked us, while our eyes were still closed, to look at our faces. Did we like the texture of our skin? What about our eyes, our eyebrows, our eyelashes, the nose, cheeks, and chin? And then, over the whole body, visualizing the shoulders,

The Entrepreneurial Woman

the arms, the elbows, the wrist, the hand, the fingers, the fingernails, and so on until I found that I could actually count all the things about my body that I loved.

Sure, when she came to the breasts, I thought, "She had to mention them, mine are overly big!" And again, when she came to the torso I found a few things I couldn't entirely love. She even asked about our hearts, lungs, livers, and other internal organs. This was really an intensive and introspective exercise.

If you can go through this exercise, you're going to find that there is more about your physical self to love than to hate! Now when you look in a mirror you can choose to see what you want to see. You can focus on your beautiful eyes rather than on the nose you've hated since you were a teenager. You can choose to believe you're beautiful! It's your thinking that influences your feelings, so if you practice thinking beautiful, you'll begin to feel beautiful. The relationship between this concept and being a successful entrepreneur is very real. If you can think, feel, and act like a success, you will radiate a glow of success that will make people want to do business with you. Everybody loves a winner! When you evidence self-assurance, others want to share it.

How many women do you know who act as though they are beautiful and so are treated that way? It all begins and ends with your definition of what you "should" look like. Get rid of the "should" and train yourself to accept and love what *is*. If there's something about your physical self that you can change, and you want to—change it! Do so-not because your husband or friends want it changed, but because you do. If you hate wearing glasses, and contact lenses will make you feel better about yourself, then get them! If a new hairstyle will make you think you're more beautiful, then get one! The key is for you to take responsibility for doing it, whatever it is! There will still be days when the pimple appears and you'll look in the mirror and say "Yuuk," but now you know the trick of looking at your eyes instead of at the pimple, and so you'll be able to snap yourself out of such negative thinking before it can get you down.

$$$

CHECKLIST FOR INTELLECTUAL SELF-IMAGE

Move quickly through the following checklist. Use a check mark beside those statements that fit your intellectual self-image.

_____I'm good at working facts into a logical order.

_____Most people I know are smarter than I am.

_____I'm good at working with ideas and developing them into a workable plan.

_____I read a lot of books.

_____I have a good memory for facts.

_____I'm terrible at math—I don't remember anything from school.

_____I'm good at reaching conclusions with a minimal amount of information.

_____I'm a question asker, critical thinker, problem solver.

_____Sometimes I feel stupid.

_____I have a hard time reaching a decision.

_____I watch too much TV.

_____I communicate well verbally and write well.

_____I can work fast and get many things done.

$$$

What about your intellectual self? Did you give yourself credit for your brains, or do you think you are stupid and unqualified? Stupid and unqualified for what? It's hard to feel self-confident if we think we are not very intelligent. Yet it's a fact that the average American woman underrates herself and her abilities to a shameful extent. She doesn't think she is as bright as she really is. The Continuum Center at Oakland University finds that

The Entrepreneurial Woman

the average wife and mother has been a support for her family for so long that she almost stops seeing herself as a person. She has been locked up in a house with small children and housework for so many years that the thought of going out into the real world with bright, competent adults scares the daylights out of her.

I suspect that if you have given yourself low grades on the intellectual checklist, you may just be expressing fear or the lack of energy required to mobilize your inherent brainpower. It is much easier to say "I can't," or "I'll try," than to actually go out and do the job.

Try to pick up an ashtray. There is no such thing as trying. You either pick it up or you don't. Try to read a book. You can't. You either read it or you don't. Similarly, you either do a job or you don't. The same holds true for intellectual ability. You can choose. You can be in charge. All you have to do is start.

Set the goal. Did you check "I watch too much TV"? Turn it off! Do you want to master numbers? Math anxiety getting to you? Identify the beast. What is it about numbers that scares you? Be specific. Is it nine times six or eight times seven that equals fifty-six? Do you think you are stupid just because you've forgotten your "nines" tables? Choose to remember it, work on it, and conquer it. It will help your intellectual self-esteem.

Even if you do make errors, that doesn't necessarily mean you're not bright enough. Learn to separate the deed from the doer. Even if you've done stupid things, don't label yourself stupid. Erase all such labels from your brain and learn from your mistakes. You're in charge, and you can choose to risk failure if the reward is great enough.

$$$

CHECKLIST FOR YOUR EMOTIONAL SELF-IMAGE

Move quickly through the following checklist. Put a check mark beside those statements that fit your emotional self-image.

Self-confidence

____I like myself.

____I like other people.

____I feel inadequate.

____I have a lot of self-confidence.

____I have a quick temper.

____I have a good sense of humor.

____I can be relaxed, even under stress.

____I feel I "should" be doing more with my life.

____I'm easily hurt by others.

____I take credit for what I do and my own strengths.

____I'm afraid to try new experiences.

____I'm proud of what I've accomplished so far in life.

____I look forward to each day.

____I worry a lot—which gets in the way of doing postive things.

$$

What about your emotional self-image? Did your answer reveal a good, strong, positive sense of self-worth, or are you unhappy with your emotional responses? Emotions are extremely powerful factors in our lives. We pick mates, careers, homes, and lifestyles because of our emotional responses, so it's essential to feel good about your emotional makeup.

Earlier, we reviewed exercises designed to improve physical and intellectual self-image. In much the same way, we can change our emotional self-image. We can choose to stop thinking negatively about ourselves.

If you fly off the handle at friends and family only to regret it later, you can change that behavior. If you hate yourself for being

The Entrepreneurial Woman

jealous over your friends' successes, you can stop being jealous. Do you have a hard time accepting compliments for what you have done and brush them aside by giving others more credit than they deserve? That's a form of self-hatred that you can choose to halt. If you worry excessively about details for fear of making a mistake, to the point where you are immobilized, you can change that as well.

Do you worry that someone else will seize upon one of your good ideas and might do it better and make more money? So what? Don't let that sort of senseless worry keep you from acting.

As an entrepreneur, you will have to strike a fine balance between emotions and cold, hard facts. Your emotions and instincts will be very helpful in your decision to open a school of the dance. But once you've made that decision, you had better put emotions aside when you negotiate the lease and sign up the workmen who will put up the mirrors and exercise bars.

If you can be positive and enthusiastic, it will affect your emotional self-image and thus build your self-confidence.

YOUR SOCIAL SELF-IMAGE

Self-confident people seem very much at ease in their relationships with others. As an entrepreneur it will be important for you to feel comfortable with customers, suppliers, employees, and contacts. The one problem seems to be that a strong, positive social self-image is so difficult to acquire today when we have been programmed from birth to believe that we are somewhat deficient socially.

How's your social self-image? Take a moment to run through the next checklist and find out. Give adequate time to each item on the list. Try to remember actual instances or situations in which you displayed the traits you recognize. It's valuable in assessing yourself. But above all, be honest! If you "fudge," you and you alone will be the loser.

$$\$$$

CHECKLIST FOR YOUR SOCIAL SELF-IMAGE

____People trust me.

____People like me.

____I have a lot of friends.

____I don't like to make a move unless my friends approve

____I'm invited to join in on many social events.

____It's important for me to belong to a club.

____I'm very stubborn.

____I'm enthusiastic with people.

____I have the ability to sell myself and my ideas.

____I have difficulty working with other people.

____I'm easily influenced by others.

____I like to be involved in projects that have social worth.

____Having the respect and admiration of others is important to me.

$$\$$$

How can you improve your social self-image? It's tough when there are so many people telling us how we are supposed to be in order to be socially well-adjusted.

You're supposed to be "the hostess with the mostest." You're supposed to join the bridge club, the garden club, the Mah-Jongg club, the gourmet club, and do well at the tennis club.

You've got to collect for the gal at the office who's getting married. You have to volunteer, throw parties, get invited.

You're supposed to read *Newsweek, Time, McCall's, MS.* and fourteen other magazines so you can hold up your end of a conversation. Mainly, though, you're supposed to fit in.

How in the world did we get this way? We've been told that we

The Entrepreneurial Woman

are worthwhile only to the extent that we have lots of friends, belong to many clubs and organizations, and have won lots of honors.

For girls, the cheerleading squad became the goal, the beauty contest the ultimate achievement. Boys, on the other hand, got different programming. They were rewarded for the mastery of skills. Look at your past experience: Would it have helped if you could kick, jump, and twirl better than any other girl if you were also acne-prone, lumpy, and possessed of a huge nose? No way! You wouldn't have made the cheerleading squad in a hundred years. Yet boys with these same deficiencies became star quarterbacks.

No wonder we lack social confidence and still look for approval from the outside. We've learned to base our achievements on society's ideals for *female* achievement rather than on our personal ideals. No wonder we're still highly sensitive to criticism! No wonder we feel guilty for "doing our own thing" in an entrepreneurial way!

How do current commercials affect you now? Do they still get in the way of your self-actualization? Do you still check for social approval before you make a move? Is the approval of your friends more important than your own achievement? If so, you are arresting your own social self-image. Thank goodness you have the strength to change. Thank goodness you can take charge.

One note comes through loud and clear as you go through your individual P-I-E-S recipe, and that is the fact that you are the *master chef*. You are in charge. You can change the behavior and attitudes that stand in the way of your precious self-confidence. The next several chapters will help you see how.

5
Learning to be assertive

I think self-awareness is probably the most important thing towards being a champion.
—Billie Jean King

Picture a day in the life of Teri, the owner of a speedy printing shop in a busy shopping center.

Teri arrives to open shop at 8:30 A.M. She's got a full day ahead of her. Fifty copies of a proposal for an architectural firm need to be found and delivered—all 200 pages of it. Her press operator has a big run of wedding invitations to get out by nine o'clock, and a service call on the Xerox machine is also scheduled that morning.

First, she decides to prepare the proposals for binding. What's this? The holes are off by a half inch. They won't fit the ring binders. "Good grief! You can't get help as you used to," she thinks, and she resigns herself to the fact that when her press operator arrives, she will have to take the proposals herself to get them repunched. (She sent a part-time worker to do it Saturday, and this was the result!)

Nine o'clock comes and goes, and no press operator. People are starting to line up in her shop. They want copies of the PTA newsletter, the Garden Club minutes, a clipping from the paper. A psychologist needs exam copies for her students, and the secretary from down the street wants copies of some letters for her boss. Teri patiently tries to help each customer in turn. The psychologist gets impatient and walks out. The copier gets stuck. Teri wonders, "Where *is* that Xerox repair person anyway?" She spends the next five minutes unjamming the machine. Finally,

The Entrepreneurial Woman

everyone's copies are run and she looks at the clock. "Oh, my God, ten o'clock already, where *is* the press operator?" She calls his home and gets no answer. She checks her answering service and finds a message from him. Seems he got stuck out in the desert during the weekend and he won't be in.

What to do now? She's got to deliver the architect's proposals for a noon presentation. She promised. The only chance she can see is to close the shop, put a note on the door, and get the copies repunched herself. Before she leaves the shop, the phone rings. It's the architect. He's mad! Teri is almost ready to cry, but she promises him he'll have the material within the hour and she quickly hangs up the phone. The Xerox person is supposed to service the machine. The wedding invitations are late. How can she leave the store? Decisions and problems seem to multiply.

Sounds like a horror story entitled, "Entrepreneurial Woman Beset by Big Business Woes." Teri has problems and they are very much like the problems you could face. Let's take a closer look at her problems to see what it takes to avoid them.

In the simplest terms, Teri lacks assertiveness. Without assertiveness, she can't set priorities, she doesn't act like a winner, she doesn't allot her time properly, and she can't communicate effectively. Furthermore, her behavior saps her self-confidence and keeps her awake nights wondering if she is really cut out to be an entrepreneur. In this chapter we will deal with each of these problems and suggest some solutions so you won't fall into a trap as Teri did.

How has she handled her priorities? She wasted an hour of her morning running copies on which she might make two cents each. She agonized over the jammed-up paper. Her priorities are all wrong. The architect's job shouldn't have been left until the last moment. She should have planned for possible foul-ups. Remember Murphy's Law: *Anything that can go wrong will go wrong.* Closing up the shop and going to do the work herself seems like the only alternative to her, but it's a poor use of her time. Couldn't she have called the place that punched the holes,

Learning to be assertive

told them of their mistake, and asked them to send a messenger for the proposals?

If she closes her shop, she will lose customers, miss the Xerox service call, and waste more valuable time messing with the machine later. If she had established her priorities earlier she could have chosen a better plan of action.

Her nonassertive communication is a huge problem. It shows in her passive acceptance of unreliable help and demanding customers. Her "Oh well, I-guess-you-can't-get-help-as-you-used-to" thought is self-defeating. If she doesn't demand good help, then she won't get it. If she doesn't communicate to her help the consequences they will have to face for poor performance, they will continue to perform poorly. Her press operator is unreliable—she should fire him and find another. Her part-time worker didn't check the holes. This is the fourth time he's made an error that has cost her more than money.

All this could have been avoided if Teri were more direct with her employees, her suppliers, and her customers. The architectural firm gave her two days to do fifty proposals. The firm always seems to have last-minute rush jobs. It makes her very nervous, but the company pays on time and gives her 200 to 500 dollars' worth of business per month. That's one boat she does not want to risk rocking.

The people who come in for Xerox copies are nickel-and-dime customers, but they demand instant service. Teri has a hard time getting them to wait their turn. Often she's in the middle of a litho run in the back room when a customer out front wants instant service. She never seems to have the right kind of help in her shop at the right time.

Teri is so fragmented that she hasn't taken the time to plan the smooth operation of her business. Planning involves setting priorities and making decisions about what's most important for the business. Until Teri values herself more, she's not going to be able to do the planning necessary to run a successful entrepreneurial venture. Teri's story is not so unusual in the life of a

The Entrepreneurial Woman

woman who's getting her business off the ground. Where should she begin? Where should you begin? Try assertiveness!

ASSERTIVENESS

Assertive behavior is open, honest, impersonal, and directed toward problem solving. It includes both verbal and nonverbal communication and takes into account the situation at hand and the other people involved. An assertive person accepts responsibility for her own feelings and doesn't blame others for what happens to her.

The difference between assertive behavior and aggressive behavior is sometimes confusing. Basically, the difference is that assertive behavior is performed in the cause of self-interest without violating the rights of others. Aggressive behavior is often thought of as "over-kill" and usually leaves another person feeling defensive, hostile, or humiliated.

A person who has acted nonassertively or aggressively in her relationships over a long period of time usually suffers from a low sense of self-esteem. Therefore, changing to assertive behavior can also lead to higher self-esteem.

Assertiveness-training courses can teach you how to feel good about yourself, how to get moving, how to relax, and how to communicate more effectively. We will look at each of these important steps toward assertive behavior individually.

FEELING GOOD ABOUT YOURSELF

In the chapter on self-confidence, we talked about avoiding negative thoughts about yourself. In assertiveness training, you learn to get in touch with what is terrific about you and your past. Participants are asked to list personal strong points and successful experiences and share them with the group. To be able to think

Learning to be assertive

like a winner and concentrate on your positive aspects, take time out right now, get a piece of paper and write down TEN THINGS I LIKE ABOUT MYSELF. Think of all the things about you that are positive. Remember, you can choose from the physical, intellectual, emotional, or social part of you.

Ann, a bookstore owner, made a list that looked like this:

1. I like my hair.
2. I like my cuddliness.
3. I like my ability to speak before a group.
4. I like my willingness to listen before I talk.
5. I like my determination.
6. I like my ability to organize.
7. I like my eyes and my smile.
8. I like my friendliness.
9. I like my sensuality.
10. I like my intelligence.

Looking at all these qualities on paper lifted Ann's self-image. She had been focusing on the negative aspects of herself for so long that she had convinced herself she was a loser. Ann, by the way, is about fifty pounds overweight and has spent fruitless (and sugarless) years dieting, losing, and gaining weight. No wonder she had lost sight of her positive aspects. Making this list really helped her reassess what she was all about and allowed her to begin taking some new risks in her business. The training class reinforced her perceptions about her friendliness, her nice smile, and her intelligence. It was her first step toward believing that she had a right to get what she wanted out of life. That's the Step Number One when you decide to become more assertive.

Another assertiveness-training technique asks participants to write down TEN THINGS I'VE DONE IN MY LIFE THAT I'M

The Entrepreneurial Woman

PROUD OF. Why don't you do that exercise too, right now?

Barbara, a widow contemplating opening her own hardware store, wrote the following list:

1. I got a job working with the forest service when I was a teenager.
2. I had three children.
3. I learned how to play the piano.
4. I went back to school and finished an accounting course.
5. I learned how to make most of the repairs needed in my house after my husband died.
6. I got a job as a part-time bookkeeper for an auto repair shop.
7. I've done the research on how to open my own small business.
8. I've saved money and invested my husband's insurance money to safeguard my future.
9. I lost thirty pounds.
10. I moved to a new neighborhood and made friends easily.

Once your list is made, you'll have a ready reference of success experiences to relive in your imagination when the going gets tough. Believe me, it's a valuable reinforcement.

GET MOVING!

An assertive person is an active person; assertive behavior is active behavior. So how do you become active after years behind a typewriter, a stove, in front of a class of kids, or at the wheel of the station wagon in the neighborhood car pool?

Get moving! Remember how important your body image is,

Learning to be assertive

and YOU are that body. The entrepreneurial body will need a lot of energy to perform the business tasks ahead, and physical activity creates energy. Get your body moving with some form of exercise.

Elva wanted to change careers but didn't know where to begin. She was just coasting along in a job she hated. She was forty-six years old and expected to work another twenty years. The motivational seminar she attended addressed the importance of energy. When one woman told how tennis had changed her life and strengthened her self-image, Elva decided there and then to sign up for a tap-dancing class. She'd always wanted to take tap-dancing as a youngster but could never afford it. Three weeks went by without mention of Elva's tap-dancing. Then, to everyone's surprise, Elva came to class with tap shoes on and demonstrated her latest accomplishments. Tap-dancing had given her the confidence to act a little "crazy." She'd spent her whole life doing conventional things until the seminar, and the dancing opened her eyes to one hidden potential.

The women in the class were excited by Elva's performance; she got a lot of reinforcement that night. By the end of the ten-week program, she was a very energetic lady. She found the energy for an evening accounting class and then set her sights on a career in her company's finance department. She'd researched the possibilities, found there was a need for more people in accounting, and followed up with action. She said she never would have had the strength for all this without the energizing intervention of tap-dancing.

Does the idea of being involved in athletic pursuits make you uneasy? Do you take a cold shower when the urge to exercise crosses your mind? Join the club, you're not alone. Most women in my training programs admit to a very low level of athletic participation. They can't remember what it feels like to work up a sweat or be out of breath from physical activity. But they do recognize the importance of adding exercise to their daily routine in order to develop the energy for assertiveness.

The Entrepreneurial Woman

You need to be able to feel how your body responds when you are under stress or tension. Once you are aware of your body, you can choose a new way of responding—with positive communications skills and reduced tension.

Remember the last time someone attacked you verbally? Maybe it was some unwarranted criticism or maybe you deserved it. How did you feel? What did your body tell you? Did you feel a sinking in your stomach? Did your hands feel clammy? Did your throat get dry? Were you stuck for words? These are the feelings you might experience every day in business when you're confronted with a difficult situation. After you've got your body moving, you'll be more aware of it. You'll know how your body feels when it's at rest, in action, or under attack. You'll recognize what's happening. Then, when your body tells you it's anxious, relaxation techniques will give you a method to help you cope while refueling your best energies.

LEARNING TO RELAX

As kids we learned to take a deep breath and count to ten to bring our emotions under control. Remember how we tried to control ourselves around a teacher or our parents when they made unreasonable requests of us? Well, that's a relaxation technique of sorts. Relaxation techniques will help you control your feelings of tension when you are frightened or immobilized by unreasonable expectations. If you learn these techniques well, you can reverse the physical symptoms of stress and tension within minutes. The goal for relaxation in assertiveness training is to help you become more comfortable *in* and more capable of coping *with* anxiety-producing situations. Some of the things you can do on your own every day are:

1. Standard loosening-up exercises in the morning before you leave home.

Learning to be assertive

2. Deep breathing exercises coordinated with the loosening-up exercises: Breathe deeply into the lower lungs while you're exercising. This will give you a "heady" feeling and will clear your mind.
3. Simple meditation exercises, like the following:
    a. In a quiet, peaceful setting, close your eyes. Empty your mind. Clear out your thoughts.
    b. Say to yourself, "I empty my mind of all anxiety, frustration, worry, anger, jealousy, hate, and irritation." Imagine these feelings flying out of your brain.
    c. Say to yourself, "I now fill my mind with calmness, peace, love, and tranquility." Picture each one coming in.
    d. Take three or four deep breaths, let your muscles relax. Imagine a peaceful, perfect day. Think the words "peace, tranquility, calmness." Open your eyes.

You can learn much more about relaxation techniques through seminars dealing with stress reduction, yoga lessons, books, your tennis coach, or your doctor.

Complete physical relaxation has a direct bearing on mental relaxation. Your mind is left clearer and less fatigued, and therefore more capable of forceful thinking. If you're mentally relaxed, little things won't unduly upset you. You might learn to "let go," not to cry over spilt milk, or not worry about water over the dam.

Many businesswomen feel that relaxation and exercise help them to think more clearly. They take yoga classes at night or play racquet-ball at lunch and return to work refreshed and ready to tackle new problems with a clear mind. Virginia, a real estate developer whose business takes her out of town a great deal, says, "Every day, when I return to my hotel room, I go through the relaxation routines and follow them up with a hot bath. It helps me concentrate and work more effectively."

LEARNING NEW BEHAVIOR

The ultimate purpose of assertiveness training is to teach you to act so that you can get what you rightfully deserve. You learn through practice and reinforcement. At the beginning, pick a situation that's not too risky. For example, you can be assertive at the dry cleaner's, for your first attempt. Think of a role model, a friend who never seems to be taken advantage of. Think how she would handle your recurrent problem: you always get your clothes back two days late with the spots just where you left them. You pay meekly, and then look for another dry cleaner, only to get the same treatment. Well, you've had enough! You resolve to get better service! You've decided to act and sound like a winner and you've even written a script for yourself.

Set the stage with these five steps: (1) identify your behavior responses in a given sitution (you're passive in this one); (2) identify how you feel about the situation (you're angry at the dry cleaner but disappointed with yourself for accepting shoddy treatment); (3) recognize the components of your behavior (you didn't look the dry cleaner in the eye, you didn't speak up and express your feeings about what was going on, you weren't spontaneous, you withheld); (4) imagine how you'll do it differently the next time (you've chosen a potentially successful experience, one with low risk, and you've written a script); (5) you've practiced this script at home, in front of a mirror, and (if you're still uneasy) with a tape recorder.

Here's your script:

Describe the Situation: "This dress still has a spot on it!"

Express Your Feelings: "I feel disappointed, especially since I want to wear this dress tomorrow."

Explain What You Want Done: "I want this dress recleaned and back here by this evening so I'll have it for tomorrow."

Learning to be assertive

State Your Bottom Line: These are the consequences you're prepared to enact if the dry cleaner doesn't give you what you want. They can be: "I'll take my business elsewhere," or "I'll report you to the Better Business Bureau," or whatever fits you best, taking into account the situation and how you feel about it. Don't lose sight of your demands.

If you'll remember positive experiences from your past when you asked for and got what you wanted, you'll be able to create a success model for yourself. You can be your own role model, relaxed, up front, and assertive. You can write the script to fit the occasion. The elements of the script are quite simple. They involve four steps and can be used just as easily in an employer-employee business confrontation. They are:

1. Describe the situation in nonjudgmental terms: "Yesterday three important projects weren't finished."
2. Express your feelings about the matter: "I was really angry when I saw they were still on the work table, especially since I'd promised them to a customer!"
3. Explain what you want done—an employee's agreement: "I need to be informed if there are going to be delays."
4. Know your bottom line (which needs to be stated only if you don't get agreement).

Does it sound like you're trying to win by intimidating? Well, there's a fine difference. First, you're not intimidating anyone. You're just asking for what you deserve and what is rightfully yours to expect as an employer. You are not forcing anyone to comply with your requests. You are allowing employees to choose whether or not they want to suffer the consequences. That's not intimidation, it's simply stating the logical consequences for a particular mode of behavior. In general, you'll find that people respect you for taking a firm stand.

COMMUNICATING ASSERTIVELY

There are other components to assertiveness that can't be ignored. These are the skills that separate assertiveness from aggressiveness and intimidation:

Your Voice: Are you talking too loudly? You don't want to yell, but on the other hand, you want to be heard. What about the pitch? Nothing turns people off more than a high, squeaky voice. Do you talk too fast? Or do you measure each word before you speak? (Sometimes, when we talk too slowly and with measured words, people think we're lying.) What about the quality of your voice? Are you whining or talking through your nose?

Your Posture: Do you stand up straight? Or do you have a slouch! What does it say about your self-confidence? When your shoulders are hunched over and your head is hanging down, you won't look assertive. How does your posture differ when you feel passive from when you feel assertive?

Gestures: If you talk with your hands, do you point your finger at people in a blaming way? Then you're being aggressive. Assertiveness is often associated with open, expansive gestures rather than with tight, closed ones.

Facial Expressions: Direct eye contact is important for assertiveness. How do you look when you're angry, sad, glad, scared? Look in the mirror. Does your facial expression fit the feeing? When you're angry, do you smile? That gives people mixed messages.

Physical Closeness: Can you shake hands? How do you feel about shaking hands with a man or woman when you meet? Assertive people are often comfortable "moving in." They're able to move a chair closer to the one in

Learning to be assertive

charge who may be hiding behind a desk, or they may be comfortable leaning forward and questioning the other person when they are negotiating for what they want.

The Words You Say: Do you stress the important words? Did you plan your verbal script to get what you want?

Remember as you embark on your new road of assertive behavior that roughly eighty percent of all communication is nonverbal. That means that people will react more to what they see than to what you say. That's why it's so important for you to be aware of the verbal and nonverbal components that express assertiveness.

HOW YOU LOOK SETS THE SCENE

You can set the scene for asserting yourself in your business by planning for the unexpected things that are going to happen! What does the way you dress say about you? If you're going to ask for money from a lender, do you want to look "successful" or do you want to look "seedy"? Do your homework. Find out about the lending officer. Is need going to enter into his decision making? Or would he rather do business with a potential winner? If so, dress like a winner, think like a winner, and look like a winner! There are other ways to set the scene in your favor.

What time of day is best for you? Are you a night person or a morning person. Again, know yourself, and "to thine own self be true." If you're a morning person, set the loan appointment for the morning, when you'll be at your sharpest. You want to present yourself as someone with a high energy level. If you slow down after lunch, that's how you'll look if you make that appointment for the afternoon. Get it? Do things that will be to your advantage! You're worth the effort! Again, you're in charge!

As you begin to practice new assertive skills, you're going to become more self-confident. It won't happen overnight, but

The Entrepreneurial Woman

within a few weeks, you'll begin to notice the difference. The goals you set at this time are important. Choose to change only one or two behavior patterns at a time. Work on these in a systematic way. Once they are integrated into who you are and they come naturally, set the goals for the next group of behavior patterns you want to change.

SETTING PRIORITIES

Do you become frantic because you have so many projects on your mind that you don't know where to turn first? Running a business requires an incredible amount of dexterity. To be successful you've got to juggle a lot of balls in the air without dropping a single one. This juggling act is particularly difficult for the woman coming out of a corporate environment with a well-defined job and lots of support or for the reentry woman with limited work experience.

All of a sudden you, and absolutely no one else, are ultimately responsible for all the details of running a successful business. You've got to worry about getting out the ad, stocking the shelves, and think about the filing, the billing, the banking. Don't forget to pick up the new stationery. Oops! We're out of stamps. What about the report? Taxes—are they due again? It all seems overwhelming at the beginning.

Relax. There's a proven technique to help you keep your head above water: Set your priorities. Learn this lesson well. It's nothing more than listing what you have to do in order of importance.

You've probably seen those cute note pads, DUMB THINGS I GOTTA DO. Well, it's not that dumb. Make a list for yourself. Only this time, write down everything that's on your mind.

Joanne had been immobilized by the responsibilities of a new business, a family, the bills, the dog, and her house. She came to class one night with her "worry" list, which looked like:

Learning to be assertive

1. I have to write a proposal for a potential client.
2. I have to follow up on a letter to XYZ Company.
3. I have to collect on three overdue invoices.
4. I have to take my dog to the vet.
5. I have to have a conference with my child's teacher.
6. I have to make a doctor's appointment for myself.
7. I have to write a technical training manual for a program I'm presenting in two months.
8. I have to get printers' bids on the training manuals.
9. I need to do grocery shopping.
10. I have to get stamps, paper clips, and tape for my office.
11. I have to invite three potential clients to lunch.
12. I have to decide on my menu for Saturday's dinner party.

Looking at the list, the class reinforced Joanne that, yes, those were real worries and might immobilize anyone. Right away Joanne started to look more hopeful. People didn't think she was crazy or stupid. They understood. Someone suggested she separate the "worry" list into two lists—home/personal and work/business—and write each list in order of importance from top to bottom. Immediately, that helped. Her lists then looked like this:

WORK/BUSINESS	HOME/PERSONAL
1. Write manual	1. Take dog to vet
2. Letter to XYZ company	2. Conference with teacher
3. Collection	3. Doctor's appointment
4. Develop and write proposals	4. Grocery shopping
5. Get printing bids on training manual	5. Decide menu
6. Get office supplies	6. Call three prospects

The Entrepreneurial Woman

Next, the group asked if Joanne could delegate any of those jobs to her children or her boyfriend. Yes, she said, the grocery shopping and office supplies shopping could be done by her teenager—but she'd still have to write out the shopping lists. The group suggested she plan the menu for Saturday night but consider foregoing dinner parties for awhile until she had her new business under control. The group also asked if one of her children could take the dog to the vet, and she said yes. Next, the group suggested she write down exactly what action needed to be taken to accomplish the remaining jobs on her lists. She did, and her task list looked like this:

1. Letter to XYZ Company: Give secretary model of ABC Company letter and make three changes (estimated amount of time needed by Joanne—five minutes).
2. Collection: Three phone calls to clients (estimated time—fifteen minutes).
3. Prospects for lunch dates: Phone calls (estimated time—fifteen minutes).
4. Making doctor appointment—five minutes; appointment—one hour.
5. Making appointment with teacher—five minutes; appointment—one hour.
6. Develop and write proposal—eight concentrated work hours.
7. Write training manual—eight concentrated work hours.
8. Get bids on training manual—can be delegated once training manual is written.

Some greater problem has been at work here too: Joanne's fear of finding out the truth, her fear of rejection. What if the clients wouldn't pay their bills? What if they weren't pleased with her work? What if the prospects didn't want to have lunch with her? What if the child's teacher had some bad news? She decided that

Learning to be assertive

these fears were merely sophisticated avoidance mechanisms.

It soon became obvious to Joanne that she was avoiding the tasks ahead of her because they looked overwhelming, and she was letting the small tasks stand in her way of getting started on the bigger ones. Preparing lists made the jobs seem more manageable and less terrifying. By getting her to be specific, the group had helped her overcome her own inertia.

Joanne learned a new term in class that night. Some of the other women had worked for corporations and knew the term—"ROI"—"Return on Investment." They advised Joanne to look for the return on investment of her time. Here's how she applied this concept. The training manual is a sure thing—she'll get paid for that—it's a job that needs to be done. She's going to get that out of the way first. On the proposal, she called the prospective client and found there were seven other firms bidding on the job, including two personal friends of company officers. She put that lower on her list of priorities. If she finishes the training manual, fine, then she'll give some time to developing a proposal for that client.

You can do the same with your own "worry" list. Bring it down to manageable size. Define the problem. Delegate. Take it step by step through the time frames of what needs to be done. Once it's down to size, it's so much easier to act on. Sometimes all the jobs on your list will take similar amounts of time and will seem equally important. Well then, go through them like the alphabet. Start at the top. Do each job and check it off your list. At the end of the day, you'll know what things need to go on tomorrow's list. You'll be organized. You'll have carefully set your priorities.

Keep your lists and review them occasionally. You will get a tremendous sense of accomplishment from looking at all the jobs you've handled. Pull them out when you need to remind yourself how terrific you really are.

Wouldn't Teri's day have been easier if she had known then what you know now?

$$$$$$$$ 6 $$$$$$$$
A woman's place is in the home …or is it?

"What's a mother to do?"

—*TV commercial*

If you feel torn, tense, anxious, or fragmented about your combined business and family responsibilities, you're not alone! For decades women have been conditioned to believe that it's their role in life to be the emotional and physical center and support of the family: the model wife, mother, and daughter. On top of those old messages, we're now being bombarded with new slogans: "You're not getting older, you're getting better," "You've come a long way, baby," and "The best man for the job may be a woman." No wonder so many of us believe we should be able to do it all! Well, if you're trying to be "supermom," throw away the cape, because the pressure of your business will get in the way of your "being there" for your family. How you can cope with these conflicts will be an individual decision, but in this chapter, we'll discuss the ways other women entrepreneurs handle these very real problems. Finding your own ways is part of the challenge.

If you're trying to hold onto the old values of home and family and run your own business, get ready for a conflict! There's hardly any way to avoid feeling "used" by your family unless you can get some cooperation from them. Maybe you can make some trade-offs—give up the kitchen to someone else in the family. Can you do it? Some women feel a loss of identity when they're no longer connected to their kitchens. "What will they need me for if they can manage the kitchen and home without

The Entrepreneurial Woman

me?" Sounds familiar? Someone has to fold the socks and fill the refrigerator. But does it ALWAYS have to be you?

What about the "truths" you've been raised on? Which ones hold you back? Which truths make you cover up your feelings because of your conditioning? Read over the following "truths." Which ones strike a nerve with you? And who says they are truths?

Who says because you are a woman:

——the kitchen is yours?

——your place is in the home?

——you're in charge of the doctors' appointments, the car pools, Sunday school, the dry cleaning, shoe repair, the hair on the soap?

——only you can plan and cook nutritious meals?

——you don't *have* to work?

——your business is just a hobby?

——you must choose between marriage and a career?

——your greatest achievement "should" be your children?

The list is interminable.

Many serious questions are being asked today about the relationships between husbands and wives and the role definitions of who does what in the home. The presence of children complicates the issue, and, unfortunately, there are no clear answers. For a businesswoman just starting her business, it's important to set priorities. Where would your husband's priorities be if he were starting a business? Probably in his business! Can you make that same commitment? What are the risks and what are your fears?

Most of the married women interviewed experienced some fears when they started their businesses. They felt that their

A woman's place

husbands, children, parents, and friends wanted them to stay as they were—and *not* change. These women were afraid of not fulfilling expectations of being "good" mothers, wives, or daughters. They also worried about being successful in their businesses and making more money than their husbands. Could they still respect and love their husbands if all this happened? They were so used to being someone's wife, mother, or daughter that the conflict of being "all they could be" frightened them. They knew how exhausting it would be to retrain their children and husbands to take over some of "mother's" tasks, and many women sometimes wondered out loud why they did it. One woman said, "Lochinvar and his castle begin to look good when things get crazy in my business and I wonder why I keep knocking my brains out to make myself a successful businesswoman."

Certainly, when the need for more money isn't the major issue, the pressure to conform to the old values is the greatest. A lot of people just won't understand why you put so much pressure on yourself if you don't need the money, so don't expect any sympathy if that's your situation. Middle- and upper-class women feel this pressure the most. Your mother may never understand why you opened a business, especially when your husband and children "need" you so much.

Marlene, forty, risked her marriage, only to gain her husband's support. She went back to law school and opened her own practice four years ago. She and Bud, her physician husband, have two daughters, aged seven and twelve, and a fourteen-year-old son. She knew when she opened her practice she'd have to work harder initially for less money than if she'd taken a job in a law firm. I asked her, "How did you find the time and energy to build up your practice while you were still running a home at the same time?"

She answered, "Who ever said I was running a home at the same time?"

She went on to tell about her husband's contribution to building the practice. When Marlene finished law school, the

The Entrepreneurial Woman

older kids were in public school, while the three-year-old was in nursery school. Her husband's practice was firmly established nearby with three other physicians; his time was more his own now than when he was building his own practice. She had supported him while he was in medical school and establishing his practice, so they agreed it was his turn now. Their combined income helped; it allowed them to hire a housekeeper. But the housework wasn't even half of the problem—it was the emotional burden of being the one whom the family leaned on.

Bud decided he could share the emotional burdens, too. When the kids' teachers called, they called Bud. When one of the kids had a dentist appointment, Bud, "Uncle Mommy," fit it into his schedule. If a car pool had to be arranged, it was "Uncle Mommy" to the rescue. Marlene could leave for her office or go to court without feeling guilty. She knew that the children's emotional needs would be looked after and that Bud would take over in the "worry department."

How did Marlene get her husband to assume these motherly responsibilities? She told the painful truth.

"It wasn't easy. Bud was the original male chauvinist, and we went through some hard times. Bud wasn't always the ideal father and husband. We've been married nearly twenty years, so you know back when we got married, the wife's role was very clearly defined as chief cook and bottle washer. I believed in the white picket fence, blue shutters, brother-and-sister outfits for the kids, and living happily ever after. I taught school for a while when Bud was in medical school. After the children were born, I subbed as a math teacher to keep my skills current. Bud would come home from his office tired and wanting to be left alone. I could understand that, knowing the pressure he worked under in a new practice and dealing with what I thought were life-and-death decisions all day. Soon, I was "the doctor's wife." I joined the auxiliary and reaped the rewards of his success, but I lost my own identity in the process. He enjoyed his new status and his practice grew. He had a life I knew almost nothing about, and I

A woman's place

began to feel our marriage was less than what I hoped for.

"He said he loved us, and he certainly provided well for us. But something was missing from my life. I had household help, so the house didn't keep me bogged down ... but I felt bogged down anyway. The baby was a year old when I decided to go back to school. I went part-time at first, and since I had worked while Bud was in med school, I felt entitled to this education and didn't give two thoughts about the expense. That's when Bud and I had our first falling out. He didn't want me spending "his" money to go back to school. I already had a profession as a teacher, a full-time job as wife and mother, so why did I need to go back to school?"

I asked, "What gave you the guts to stand up to your husband? Weren't you scared of rocking the boat?"

She answered, "Of course, I was scared. But I also recognized that I was drowning in inactivity, feeling low about myself. And if I felt this way about myself, Bud, at some level, was also feeling the same way about me. I really didn't have a choice. I decided the risk was worth it. The worst that could happen was that he'd divorce me, and I'd be a well-taken-care-of ex-Mrs. Doctor. I knew we had a lot at stake in our marriage, the love we had for each other surfaced every now and then, we had great times on vacations, and we both loved the children. I decided to gamble ... that's all!"

I was struck by her courage and asked, "When did it all turn around for you? When did he become so supportive?"

She answered, "Once I hit my stride in law school, I began to get good grades, feel more energetic, and like myself more. Bud, too, could see the positive change in me, and he became more interested in what was happening to me during my day. My enthusiasm for this new stage of my life gave me a real lift. I guess at some level Bud had outgrown me, but neither of us was willing to admit it. Now he could see me growing and becoming a more interesting person. He hates to admit it, but I chose the right path for me, which became the right path for him too. Now it's a

The Entrepreneurial Woman

shared thing. We're both enthusiastic about my career, and it's rubbed off on the kids. They now talk about their 'Mommy the lawyer,' and their 'Uncle Mommy the doctor.'"

Is life really that perfect for her?

"No," Marlene says, "it's not. I still have problems with my image of what a woman should be and should be doing. There are days when I'm totally unavailable to my family, and I feel moments of guilt. When Bud's the only parent watching our daughter in a school play, I sometimes wonder what the other mothers think. Do they think our daughter is 'poor Susan with the crazy mother'? These moments are fleeting, however. Our son, who's fourteen, is also a royal pain in the neck about my work. He's turned into a male chauvinist and constantly tries to bait me. He has a hard time with the fact that his mother is a lawyer. I know it's just a phase of adolescence—a phase he'll definitely get through—but it gets to me anyway."

Even with the supportive husband, Marlene's life is still not all roses. There are many nights when she's too exhausted to talk to anyone, let alone be civil at the table. Her sex life sometimes suffers, and her husband doesn't always understand. The temptation to give it all up sometimes overwhelms her, but still she hangs in there. Her story reinforces the belief held by many women that it will never be perfect. Some days things will be great, and then some days we'll feel like we're just able to keep our heads above all that water.

Marlene's story also illustrates a major problem faced by many women entrepreneurs today: how to get their husbands on their team. Marlene got Bud's support and thus was relieved of a major part of the burden of taking care of their children. She took herself seriously and declared her priorities no matter what the risk may have been to her marriage.

Other women have chosen different strategies for handling a business and their homes at the same time. Some have been successful and others haven't. Let's meet a few of these women and find out what they've done.

WORKING AT HOME

Louise has run a public relations business from her home for about a year.

The first thing that struck me about Louise when we talked was that she looked so tired. We met in her home "office," a room off the kitchen that had been built as a maid's room. The fact that her office was in the maid's room was in itself an irony. Her children were in school all day, but the remnants of their morning departure were evident in the kitchen—strawberry jam sticking to the counters, dishes in the sink, an empty milk carton on the table, along with two coffee cups and the morning paper. The mess didn't seem to bother Louise and she made no apologies for it. She had given up ownership of the kitchen! But as she began to talk, her voice showed doubt as to whether she would be able to continue in her business if it meant continuing to work at home. This is what she said.

"Working at home seemed like the ideal solution to me . . . we had this extra room, I could install a business phone, and if there was an emergency with the kids I was close by. Why spend the extra money on an office? But it's driving me crazy. I feel like a warden to my plants. The dustballs under the bed tyrannize me, the phone interrupts me with idiotic sales pitches and surveys all day long, and on top of that, when the kids come home, "Mommy" is totally available. They don't see me as a working professional. I don't understand how my neighbor's husband can work at home so successfully . . . it must be because she runs interference for him and he's able to separate himself emotionally from the home. I know I can't."

Louise called me a few months later to tell me she'd rented a small office near her home, which, she said, gave her a sense of going to work. "It separates me physically from the home. I needed a different environment. It's very energizing. It's amazing, but knowing I'm paying for this office makes me work harder and go after clients more aggressively."

The Entrepreneurial Woman

But how was her care of the home and the children working out? "The house is still a mess most of the time, but the whole family agreed to clean it every Saturday. I guess we're just not as particular as other people, although every now and then my husband and I get annoyed by the kids' mess. It's hard for me to be positive and not notice the peanut butter smears on the table, the newspapers all over the floor, and to thank my son for feeding the dog. Sometimes I do tend to nag . . . but I'm only human. The saving thing, however, is that our bedroom is off limits to the kids, so it's pretty clean and my husband and I retreat there a lot when we are home at night. The kids are getting somewhat upset when they want to bring friends home and the place is a mess, so I've given them permission to clean up if it bothers them. I think they're beginning to get the message, but, believe me *it's hard!*"

When Louise was working in her home, she seemed to suffer from the malaise that affects so many women working from their homes. The lack of a standard nine-to-five day and an office to go to gives some women the feeling that they're not really doing anything, that they're not really working. When they're at home, it's so easy to neglect their work for "women's work" and get hooked in the webs of macrame plant-holders. Even though some of us can create the energy to work in our homes, make the calls, do the books, and so on, we somehow still manage to put ourselves down when our schedules allow a "woman's life." Separating the domestic from the professional role is twice as hard for the woman running her business out of her home.

For Louise, the working-at-home solution didn't work, but other women have made a go of it.

Shelagh Moore operates Shelagh's Greenhouse, a plant-sales-and-care business, from her home on the Palos Verdes Peninsula. She's been in business for three years and gets lots of financial and emotional rewards from her business. Here's how she worked it out.

"I started my business three years ago with plant parties in people's homes. I'd go to the nursery, get several plants, and then drag them to the party. The hostess would get a free plant, for which she would invite her friends and serve coffee and cake. I'd buy the plants wholesale and resell them slightly below retail, so the women were getting a good deal. After about a year I was running out of women who would hostess my plant parties and I recognized that in order to grow, I had to expand my base of operations to other neighborhoods. My home and children are an important part of my life, and I knew that if my business grew too much, I would have less time with them. I didn't want to stretch myself that way, so I decided to investigate other options. I made a list of what I had going for me and found I had a pretty impressive list of positives. I had suppliers who knew me, I had credit, I had satisfied customers who called me for more plants, and I had a way with plants and their care and feeding.

"I was having lunch in a neighborhood restaurant one day when I noticed its plants. They were a mess! Then it hit me, CARE AND FEEDING! That was it! I decided to put my 'positives' to work, and at that very moment, before my courage vanished, I spoke to the owner. I told him of my plant service, my idea to get new plants for his restaurant, to save those I could, and to set up a weekly care schedule to keep his plants looking well. He seemed interested in the idea, and asked what I would charge. I didn't have the foggiest idea, but I didn't let him know that. I gulped, and said, 'I'll figure out an estimate and get back to you before 5 P.M.' I got the contract and uncovered a new source of business.

"All the restaurants in my neighborhood seemed to have trouble keeping their plants healthy, so I knew where to sell my service. Now I have contracts from several large restaurants and businesses in the area. I've built a small greenhouse at home where I grow plants from cuttings, and I get great enjoyment from this new phase of my business."

How does she handle the pressure of home and children along with her business?

"I've purposely kept my business down to a manageable size. I don't want it to interfere with my job as a mother. My

The Entrepreneurial Woman

children are very important to me and will be gone in a few years. While they're still young—they are seven and ten—I consider this business a learning phase of my life. I've got lots of time and I know I want to use these years wisely. That way, if I want to go into business in a bigger way when they're grown, I'll have the experience and track record to make it happen! But it is sometimes hard to resist the urge to get bigger. Recently I turned down a ten-restaurant chain because it would have taken me too far from home to be here after school for the children."

Shelagh seemed so calm; I couldn't help asking, "Are you able to keep your house, be there for your children, and run a business by yourself, with no help? She answered, "No, I get help from my children, my husband, and I have a woman come in to clean every other week. But, I'm very well-organized and we're basically a neat family. In the morning the kids make their beds before leaving for school, bring their dirty clothes downstairs, we all rinse off our own breakfast dishes, and that's all there is to it."

Knowing kids, there had to be more to the story than that, so she went on to tell me, "The kids want a van, and so do I. It will help with my business, and we'll have it for family camping trips. This way, when the kids work around the house or help me deliver plants after school, they know they are earning a seat in our van." Obviously, Shelagh had spent some valuable time training her kids to help themselves when they were still very young.

Shelagh's experience shows that combining a home and business with family responsibilities can be done. But it takes organization and a clear set of priorities to run a business out of a home successfully.

HIRING HELP

Elaine's been in business for herself the last seven years, but she's always been a "working mother." Her children are now eleven and thirteen years old, and pretty self-sufficient. She has two

A woman's place

dogs, two cats, is a gourmet cook, and a very successful businesswoman. Her job is very demanding, as she runs a consulting business and an employment agency. She has eighteen employees and last year did close to a half-million dollars in business. She solves the problems of being wife, mother, and entrepreneur the same way she solves her business problems. She hires the best employees she can find and pays them well.

"I've always had a substitute mother to fill in for me. I just look for the most qualified candidate for the job. I pay well, offer decent working conditions, and expect to get what I pay for."

She went on to say, "The women who have been in charge of my kids are hired to do just that. They're expected to take the kids to the doctor, to the dentist, to their music lessons, and to be on call if one of them gets sick at school and needs to be picked up. For that I pay a good weekly salary, vacation pay, and social security. I believe you can find a competent mother substitute. You have to be willing to pay for it."

ENLISTING GRANDPARENTS

Linda's been divorced for twelve years, and her children were both under three when she started her business. She talked about those early years.

"My Mom and Dad lived close by and would come to take the kids whenever I'd let them. I was an only child and could do no wrong in my parents' eyes. When I was divorced, they thought the world had come to an end for their darling little daughter, and they meant to make it up to me and not let me or my children suffer. Looking back on it, I guess my predicament allowed me to give up my responsibility as a nurturing parent so I could make money to support those two kids—somebody had to do it! The thing that got to me though, was the constant mess in my house. I never had time to pick up or to put things away. My parents spoiled the kids and kept giving them more things. I finally

The Entrepreneurial Woman

resigned myself to living in a disorderly house as long as I could go to my orderly office. I'd close my eyes when I came home at night and if I tripped over a toy, I pretended not to notice.

"I remember those early years as being very tense. I was on edge all the time. It's a good thing my parents were around to give the kids love and attention, because I had very little left to give at the end of each day with all the pressures I had.

"I started out as a residential real estate saleswoman. I soon got my broker's license because the only way to make real money in this business is to own your own firm. The problems I faced in setting up my business were tremendous, and getting listings was only half of it. I had to learn how to hire people, do the books, do PR, become visible in my community, and so on. Now, it's easier to manage. My boys are pretty self-sufficient, and the business fits into my life. I'd never advise anyone with small babies to do what I did. I'm just glad I had my parents around to help, though it would have been so much easier to get a job with regular hours. If I had to do it over again though, I'd probably still choose the same road. I guess I'm slightly crazy, but I love being my own boss and calling the shots."

Linda had given up a lot of her youth getting her business off the ground, so I asked her about that aspect. She answered, "I'm thirty-five now, and for the past five years I've had a man in my life again. We're getting married this spring, so I don't feel I've given up anything. For the first few years after my divorce, I was so angry at all men that it was good not to have time for a social life. When my friend came along, I was ready to get involved. He's also very interested in my business and excited about what I've accomplished. Our dream is that one day we might combine his business expertise with mine and start something that is 'ours.' We'll first see how this business progresses. But let me say, my parents are still breathing a sigh of relief that their little girl will be a married lady after all!"

It sounds like Linda's getting a supportive husband in the bargain. Entrepreneurial women can have it all!

ENLISTING THE FAMILY

Kathy decided to enlist the help of her teenagers when she opened her tennis shop a few years ago. She planned for family support as if the opening of her business were the Normandy invasion. After the first few months, however, all the charts and agreements with the kids began to break down. This is the story she told.

"My whole family plays tennis, so when I said I was opening up a tennis shop everyone was enthusiastic. They could see tennis clothes at a discount, all the latest equipment, and free balls in their future. They weren't really prepared, however, for unwashed clothes, the empty refrigerator, the unmade beds, and no dinner in the oven. They'd all agreed to help with the chores around the house. Each had diligently filled out the blank spaces on the weekly chart. But their help soon turned to forgetfulness, and I was getting angry. I knew I'd have to do something drastic. So I went on strike! All the things I'd been doing to make up for their forgetfulness were left undone—and they began to notice what needed doing! The first day, when my teenage son, Billy, had no socks to wear to school, he yelled, 'Mom, where are my socks!' And you know what? 'Mom' didn't answer. Soon, they all got the message and we decided to have a family meeting. My husband, who thought that my business wouldn't interfere with his creature comforts, was also part of this summit meeting.

"We talked and talked, and finally came to the following conclusions. 'Daddy' would strip the beds on Monday morning before he left for work and start the sheets in the washer. He'd also wash the breakfast dishes two mornings a week. Debbie would dry the sheets and remake the beds when she got home from school on Monday, and Billy would vacuum and empty the dishwasher twice a week. Nancy, the ten-year-old, would be in charge of feeding the dog and cat, walking the dog, and taking out the newspapers and garbage daily. Each child also agreed to take total responsibility for keeping his or her own room neat. That left

The Entrepreneurial Woman

me with the grocery shopping, the laundry, and preparing dinner. I thought that was still too much for me alone, and I told them so. We resolved that my husband and I would both do the weekly shopping at night. I would plan the meals, and the kids would take turns washing the towels and other sturdy washables. I would handle the delicate clothes, and have someone come in to help with cleaning and ironing one day a week.

"Now, whoever gets home first starts dinner, and sometimes I even walk in at 6:30 to see my husband busily chopping the vegetables. So far it's working, but of course there are still days when the kids forget to make their beds or help when dinner is late. But generally, the kids pitch in and help."

She went on to say, "The thing I hate, though, is that I'm still in charge of working it all out. I wish someone understood how I felt! It just isn't fair. It's hard to be mad at my husband . . . after all, most of his friends have wives who take care of them and don't demand any help with the house. The rules have changed around here though, and I guess I'm lucky they cooperate this much."

It sounded as if Kathy did succeed in getting it all together. She even has her two teenagers working in the store a few afternoons a week, and she mentions that this gives them a real understanding of the pressure involved in running a business. Having her kids helping out at the store reminded me of the small stores in my childhood neighborhood. Most of the kids went to Mom and Pop's store after school where they were expected to help out. And they did! Well, drafting the family is still an option for some entrepreneurial women.

BRINGING THE KIDS ALONG

Lesley tells this story: "My fabric shops were a going concern when I got pregnant with our last child. I started this business seven years ago when my other two children were in school. Now my husband

A woman's place

has joined the business, and we have four stores."

How had she worked this out as the mother of two active youngsters? She explained: "Kurt and Grace were five and seven when I opened my first store. The store was close to their school, so they could just walk over after school. My business met a need in our neighborhood. Right from the beginning I had more business than I could handle alone, so I hired a woman to help out in the store. So if there was ever an emergency with the kids at school I could get there. I also had a good list of sitters I could call on at a moment's notice if one of the kids was sick and needed to stay home from school."

Her strategy changed after child number three was born three years ago, and her husband came into the business.

She said, "At the beginning, I went into business thinking this was something that could keep me busy when the kids were at school. I never realized how fast I'd get hooked into making money. The business took off, and I learned so much that first year that it seemed a shame to just waste it in one store. My husband and I talked it over, and he figured he'd live longer working for something that was ours rather than spending the rest of his life on someone else's payroll."

Listening to this story I couldn't help but think, "All those years of making dinner—but give a woman just one year of making *money!*"

She went on, "Anyway, when Joe came into the business, we planned the opening of our second store in a way I'd never planned our first. I found it amazing to see how he researched the location, negotiated the rent, shopped for equipment, and hired help. He did it just the way the 'How to Start Your Own Business' books say it should be done. I did the same things when we opened our third and fourth stores. 'Just about the time we opened our third store, Annie was born. My husband and I decided I was too important to the business to stay home with her as I'd done with the other two. So, we just brought her along! That's one of the nicest things about working for yourself—you

The Entrepreneurial Woman

can do what you want to do! I kept a port-a-crib in the back room and she slept most of the day when she was an infant. As she grew, we traded the port-a-crib for a playpen, and Annie became somewhat of a novelty in our shop. The employees loved her, and since she never knew any other way of being a baby, she adjusted. We kept a playpen in each store, so wherever we had to be that day, Annie could come along.

"In the beginning, Annie would always come with me, but as she got older and more active, Joe took her with him as often as I did. We were pretty loose about it, and it seemed to work out. When she grew tired of being in a playpen, one of us or an employee would take her out for a walk around the shopping center. The other merchants got to know her, and her visits became a treat for most of them. She started nursery school when she was two-and-a-half, and then we found a wonderful Montessori school for her where she goes from 8 A.M. to 4 P.M. each day. She seems to love it. The other children are pretty busy with after-school activities now, but they check in with Joe or me to let us know where they'll be. Since hardly anyone is ever at home these days, the place stays pretty clean. I've found a once-a-week cleaning service is all we need."

Lesley and Joe seem to have worked out the problems of combining home and entrepreneurship in a suitable way.

OTHER PROBLEMS

Kids and nonsupportive husbands can really slow you down when you are trying to launch your new venture. But just because you have handled them and they're securely out of the way, don't think your problems are over. There are other people ready to take potshots at you; others, who for some reason have made your life their project and have their own expectations as to how you "should" be.

"What, you're opening a boutique? Who'll watch my

A woman's place

grandchildren? You've got a beautiful home, a loving husband, and three children—what else do you want? Doesn't my son make enough money to support you? Why do you need to have a business?"

These words, or variations on the same theme, have been uttered to just about every married entrepreneur interviewed in the preparation of this book. It is very hard for the mothers of most of today's businesswomen to understand their daughters' motivations. Our new independence may be too big a threat to their fragile egos and the choices they've made in their lives. So, if Mom tries to instill this type of guilt in you, you'll just have to humor her. Tell her it's part of your mid-life crisis, that times are changing, or that it's a way for you to travel, write-off expenses, or save money on your wardrobe now that you'll get it wholesale!

What you say to Mother is less important than your recognition of what's happening—basically a clash in values. In these times of transition, your mother may not understand why you do what you do. It was easy enough for her to understand why you took an office job. You needed the money. (Mother always said you should have "mad" money.) But that was just a job, and it left you enough time during the day to talk to her on the phone, gave you the energy to have her to dinner a few times a month, and left you the time to be available as a good daughter or daughter-in-law should be. Now with this store you're opening—you won't have time for anyone! How selfish can you get?

That's the word that does affect some of us. SELFISH! We're getting back to the concept of valuing ourselves enough to choose what's right for us. Nothing is as healthy as healthy self-interest! And that's very different from selfishness!

Old friends, too, may react in much the same way as Mother. Some won't understand why you are deserting them, no matter what you say. They may be hurt and let you know it. Friends change, and you may find that you and your friends are drifting apart as your business interest and expertise grow. New friends will probably take the place of the old ones who drift away

The Entrepreneurial Woman

and the new ones will most probably be in business themselves. Professional and entrepreneurial women talk about the inevitability of tension between old friends as one of the group begins to change and grow professionally. You may have a new identity in their eyes, and sometimes they'll sense that as threatening. You'll be measuring yourself by what you're accomplishing and learning in your new business, and your friends' opinions won't carry as much weight as they used to. You'll be tied up with business pressures and your time will be more precious to you. No longer will you be able to talk away half the day on the phone, and many old friends will feel betrayed.

It may be painful to see this happening, and you may be torn by the guilt of letting your friends down, but if you're committed to your business, that's where your priorities must stay. One woman who feels the loss of old friends acutely, but is totally tied up in her work for the next year, told her close friends, "Just consider I'm in Europe for the year, and having too marvelous a time to write."

As an entrepreneurial woman, you'll find yourself overwhelmed by work some weeks—it'll come in spurts, when you'll have no time for your private life. But there will be slack periods too, time to catch up with family and friends. All the relationship problems you may have will be a real test of how much you value yourself and how determined you are to hang in there.

Another real test will emerge the day your husband decides to "help" you in your business. Are you going to pay him a salary? Is he going to be full-time or part-time? If you're going to pay him, will you pay him as much as or more than the employees who've been with you since the beginning?

These and other issues need to be settled before your husband comes to "lend a hand" in the business. It's still basically a man-woman thing and even though you feel like you're totally equal in the home, it's different in the business world! Can his ego take being Number Two? Can *your* ego take being Number One? Are you frightened of seeing him in a

A woman's place

Number Two position? Face it, he can't be an equal in your business if you started it and built it without him. Your employees look at you as "the Boss" and that may be a heavy psychological hurdle for your husband to handle. He'll feel an ownership too, in the business. After all, he's probably been a part of its growth on an emotional and psychological level, even though he may not have been physically present. You don't want to destroy your communication or your relationship, so make sure you've settled the man-woman thing at home before you bring your husband into your business.

Listen to Jon, a husband involved in his wife's business:

"I came into the business in an area nobody was handling, so I wasn't taking anyone's job away. I was going to clean up the Accounts Receivable, to find out why people weren't paying. At first the office manager felt threatened. She wanted to know what I was doing there. Accounts Receivable gets into all phases of the business. When I located the breakdown, I had to problem-solve, but I maintained a very low profile. I specifically chose to play the Number Two position. Mine was an investigative role and I knew I would find things about the business that might threaten other employees, so I decided to just learn all I could and be helpful. Instead of criticizing, I devised new systems for collection and helped the office manager introduce them to the staff.

"It's interesting, but there's less goofing around by the employees on the days that I'm there. Maybe they think Big Brother is watching them. I found, though, that I really needed to keep my reactions under control. My wife was the boss, and I couldn't disturb that image with her employees. There were times when I really wanted to shake up some of them. They were doing things in such an incompetent manner, but I checked myself. After all, in their eyes, it's her business, not mine. The bottom line, though, is that this business of hers is building us a secure financial future."

It may not be easy to integrate your husband into your business, and what works for some entrepreneurial women may not work for you.

$$$$$$$ 7 $$$$$$$
Stress and the entrepreneurial woman

*There is only so much you can learn
about skydiving from standing on the ground.*
—Joyce Maynard

Six weeks of pneumonia was not what I expected as a reward for starting my second business!" Dale Jensen related her experiences to me a few months after she had opened a women's sportswear store in a large shopping center.

"I burned the candle at both ends, tried to do everything I used to do. I had a jewelry business for two years, and I thought I knew all about the pressures. But I wasn't ready for this! In my old business I had a partner, so I could keep my homemaker identity intact. I went to the jewelry market once a week to buy, set up appointments with customers, kept the books, and still served dinner on time every night. I figured I need only add the things that had to be done for the second business—the buying, the bookkeeping, managing the shop seven days a week, and hiring and training help. I didn't give up my Wednesday tennis game or my job as chief cook and bottle washer at home. In a month I felt enormous pressure. My body gave out. But even when I became ill I still couldn't relax. I went back to the shop too soon and as a result almost had to be tied to the bed until I got well."

Dale's story illustrates how susceptible the body can be to the pressures faced by entrepreneurial women. I've talked with women who developed backaches, insomnia, arthritis, acne, ulcers, migraine headaches, asthma, and anxiety from the stress of developing a business. Dale's illness is a textbook case of what

The Entrepreneurial Woman

can happen to a person under such stress. Her body lacked the reserve of energy necessary to ward off infection, and when she contracted pneumonia she simply did not have the strength to fight it.

What is stress? The word was borrowed from physics about forty years ago by Dr. Hans Selye of the University of Montreal to describe the body's response to overloading the system with too many outside stimuli or pressures.

If you think of the body as a spring, it will illustrate what stress can do to us. If the spring is pulled and stretched within its limits, it will bounce right back. But pull it too far and it will snap. That's what happens to our bodies—too much stress and we're liable to snap.

In the last chapter we discussed family situations that can cause conflict. Role conflict, necessitating a frantic type of juggling act, is just one form of pressure that entrepreneurial women face. Half the problem in managing stress is pinpointing the cause.

To an entrepreneur, any or all of the following can cause stress: financial insecurity, an uncertain future, decisions, deadlines, due dates, a conflict of values and ethics, an overload of information, or no access to information.

Not everyone reacts to stress in the same way. The pressures involved in doing things we enjoy are not stress-producing. It is frustration and conflict that produce stress reactions.

Loré Caulfield, owner of Loré's Lingerie, learned the meaning of stress on a trip to Dallas. She had an appointment with the lingerie buyer at Neiman-Marcus, and since her business was just getting started, a great deal depended on her success. Loré tells it this way.

"My sales manager and I were late for the plane and were rushing to the gate. I noticed that there were two planes at the same gate, but we flashed our boarding passes, boarded the plane we were directed to, and within minutes it taxied down the runway and we took off. Not long after we were airborne I realized we were on our way to New York, not Dallas!

"My first response was panic! All our luggage and most of our samples were on the plane headed for Dallas. I was due at Neiman-Marcus at two the following afternoon. What to do?

"Word quickly spread through the plane with the captain's announcement about the two 'frazzled' ladies on the wrong plane. That made me angry! It was clearly the airline's mistake and not ours! It may have been a joke to him, but it was a catastrophe for us.

"I decided to make the best of a terrible situation. The shot of adrenaline I felt in my initial panic energized me. Why not use this twist of fate to my advantage? I had a carry-on case that contained a few pairs of silk bikinis and some other small items from my line. I made a mental note of how much money it would cost me to make a sales trip to New York, how much energy I'd have to use in planning it, how many phone calls and letters it would take to set it up, and I decided to go for broke. We would include New York in our sales itinerary, and the airline would foot the bill.

"We landed in New York in the early hours of the morning and the airline agreed to put us up overnight in a hotel near the airport. After much insisting on our part, the airline also agreed to pay our expenses in New York and put us on an afternoon plane to Dallas. That left us the morning to make our business calls.

"Picture this: two women, no luggage, no makeup cases, nothing to sleep in, no toothbrushes, and no hair-dryers for the obligatory morning shampoo. Add to this the time change from Los Angeles to New York, the effects of jet lag, the effect on our clothes of sitting in a plane for five hours, and you'll get a clear picture of what we looked like—two street urchins! Now, picture these two urchins showing up to sell a very expensive line of silk lingerie to the highest quality stores in New York. Well, we did it, and this is how.

"The first thing in the morning I called Dallas and changed

The Entrepreneurial Woman

our appointment to the next day. Then I called the lingerie buyers from the top stores in New York. Miracle of miracles, I was able to set up three appointments for that day before our plane left for Dallas! I guess the buyers were fascinated by my story and the incredible turn of events that had brought us to New York. By now I was feeling it was wonderful! We went to Bonwit Teller, Saks Fifth Avenue, and Bergdorf Goodman—and sold to them all. We even had time for a glorious luncheon celebration, courtesy of the airline, before we left for Dallas.

"We were so high with our New York experience that when we got on the plane to Dallas we felt we could fly without its engines. We felt so successful that there was no way we could fail in Dallas. And we didn't—we sold Neiman-Marcus a good initial order. Now my silk lingerie is in all the finest stores in the world.

"Every time I think of that experience, it gives me new energy. Even with all the stress and pressures of being in business, I wouldn't trade it for another way of life. My business has doubled in volume this past year and when I think that the plane trip of two years ago was the turning point for us, I have to laugh. I only wish that the airlines captain who thought we were so 'frazzled' could know of our success."

Loré's story shows how self-confidence can go a long way toward avoiding poor stress reactions; a less confident woman might have capitulated when confronted with the same problem.

Helene is an educational consultant who puts in many exhausting ten-hour days, but has had no stress symptoms. This is how she describes her week:

"Monday, I flew to Chicago. I met with several potential clients on Tuesday and Wednesday. Wednesday night, I flew to St. Louis to present a two-day seminar. I stayed with friends in St. Louis and spent the nights catching up on old times. While it was marvelous seeing my friends, I got no more than five hours sleep on Wednesday and Thursday. Friday night I flew back to Los Angeles and slept a little on the plane. On Saturday I was going again at top speed. I went bicycling with an old friend for about two and a half hours. Saturday night I went to a dinner party for my cousin's fortieth birthday, and Sunday I worked out an approach for some new business with one of my associates. It's all so energizing that I wouldn't give up any of it. I'd never be happy with a less hectic schedule."

Helene is also on a regular exercise program that forces her to relax. As she puts it, "I find that after half an hour of heavy exercise I'm so tired that I just have to sit and stare at the walls for awhile."

Through this process, Helene is recharging her body—whether she knows it or not.

Stress researchers in Great Britain have found that exercising two or three times a week for as little as fifteen minutes at a time aids resistance to stress. The best exercises for this, they found, are swimming, running, bicycling, and calisthenics. Helene's bicycling, in addition to her regular exercise program, helps her to eliminate stress.

Of course, as Dr. Selye points out, a certain amount of stress is beneficial to well-being. We should not aim to avoid stress completely, but we should learn how to recognize our individual responses to it and then work to change our lives accordingly. Dr. Selye also believes that a positive attitude can turn a negative stress, one that produces illness, into a positive one—what he calls "eustress." He coined this word for healthy stress, the kind that can energize. Loré's positive attitude allowed her to turn distress into eustress.

Dr. Selye also believes there are two types of people: "racehorses" and "turtles." Racehorses are people who are happy with a fast-paced lifestyle. They are always involved in one project or another and never slow down. They thrive on stress. Turtles, on the other hand, require peace and quiet. According to Dr. Selye, stress occurs when a turtle goes for the Kentucky Derby or a racehorse becomes a librarian.

I asked Dale and Helene whether they were racehorses or

The Entrepreneurial Woman

turtles according to Dr. Selye's definition and whether they had positive or negative attitudes toward business pressures.

Helene described her earlier life to me. "I was voted 'most likely to succeed' and can't remember a time when I wasn't actively involved in something. I think I'm just a natural overachiever. Even when I was a little girl, I was the one who organized the backyard stage shows. I'm not happy unless I'm busy. My parents were the same way—they were always involved in many projects."

Dale talked about her earlier life: "I was never a quiet kid. I was always in a hurry. My kids are the same, never still, always on the run."

Clearly, both Helene and Dale were racehorses. Then why did all this activity suddenly get Dale down? She talked about her pneumonia. "I'd always gotten away with putting a lot of pressure on myself, but I guess this time I just wasn't prepared to fight off the bug that bit me. I was without a partner, and some of the problems with my new business really got me down. For instance, I needed some golf socks and I called a New York supplier long distance. I told him I wanted two hundred dollars' worth of socks, and asked him to ship the order COD or, if necessary, I'd send the money first. Three weeks later I received a form letter asking for my credit history. I was really angry. I needed those socks and I couldn't understand how they could treat a customer that way! I was also having trouble finding reliable help. I hired about five different part-time workers before I got sick, and each one was worse than the last. I fired them all, one by one. Getting sick was probably my body's way of telling me how much I disliked what was going on!"

That was the answer. Helene's enthusiasm and positive view of her work pressures created eustress, while Dale's negative experiences created distress. Eustress can energize you and help you through a hectic schedule like Helene's, but the distress of negative feelings and pressures can cause a physical breakdown like Dale's.

Stress

What about turtles—can they cope with the stresses of entrepreneurship? Do they handle the reactions to stress any differently?

Gloria owns a small nursery near Dale's shop, called Whispering Ferns. Gloria is a quiet, calm woman who derives great pleasure from her plants and her shop. She has no tolerance for stress and does not acknowledge its existence. She expresses only positive feelings about her business and her beautiful plants. Her early life fits Selye's description of a turtle, and she certainly has found a business that fits her personality. She has no desire to expand; she loves her small business just the way it is, and is satisfied with what she earns from it.

What if you're a low-pressure person and you want to start a high-powered business, one that requires constant activity and a demanding schedule? Will you be able to make it? It's easier to come to terms with what and who you are than to change long-term patterns. However, if you feel those patterns no longer work for you, then give yourself permission to try to change them. Weigh the choices. Ask youself, "If I change, what price will I have to pay? Is it worth it?" The conflict of change itself may cause stress and thus indicate that it's time to take it easy and integrate the new you into who you already are.

Karen was a straight A student in school, a quiet, calm, and orderly young lady. She's been in business for herself for the past seven years. When I asked her how she has learned to cope in the world of business, she said, "It's an effort, but I do it. Every time I have to make a strong point with a customer, I die a little inside. I often feel it would be easier to go home and crawl under the covers, but the pressure of meeting that payroll every Friday keeps me motivated. Even after all these years, I still have to push myself to be aggressive. It puts me under a lot of stress, but it's worth it. I've grown so much, and I know the change is for the better. And besides, the business is making money now." Karen enjoys her growth, and her positive attitude allows her to escape the ill effects of stress.

The Entrepreneurial Woman

Lack of working capital is often a major cause of stress. One business-woman told of how she broke through the barrier of financing for a woman. She recalled the elation she first felt when the bank granted her a loan of $200,000. It would allow her to expand her business, promote a new product, and grow nationally in scope. She was pleased that the bank had so much confidence in her. But then the novelty wore off, and reality sank in. She *owed* $200,000! Sleepless nights, cold sweats, and a palpitating heart began to torment her. Her financial worries got in the way of her creativity, so that she could no longer think clearly about the new product she wanted to promote. This conflict caused a stress response, and she realized she must get some relief. She knew the constant worry was taking its toll, and she couldn't afford to be sick, so she adopted a plan of exercise to relieve the stress and take her mind off her problems. Now she goes ice skating three times a week at lunchtime and is doing her yoga exercises faithfully. She is able to sleep nights again, and she is beginning to analyze her priorities.

How can you tell if you're under stress? You may not even be aware of it—but your body knows. Your heart rate may increase and you may show an increased amount of physical activity.

There are other signs. Do you find yourself talking in fragments—starting a second sentence before you've finished the first? Are you intensely ambitious, competitive, and anxiously aware of time? Do you feel guilty when you do absolutely nothing for a few days? Do you put yourself under pressure by trying to do too many things at one time? Do you schedule appointments one on top of another, trying to see as many people as possible in one day, have a hard time listening to things that don't interest you, eat fast? Are you compulsive about being the first to get things done? Do you know you're working too hard and putting yourself under too much pressure?

If you can answer "Yes" to any of the above questions, you're exhibiting signs of stress. Such patterns of behavior can overload your system and may even endanger your health.

Stress

Marilyn Baxter, the owner of Calliope, Inc., a publishing and research firm in Los Angeles, found herself in a state of acute anxiety. Before she recognized the effect that a stressful life was having on her she had suffered tachycardia twice. And at the age of thirty-five! She'd been in business for six years, her business was successful, but the pressures of getting through the lean periods, dissolving a partnership, and meeting a weekly payroll were taking their toll. She found that she had high blood pressure, although the doctors could find no reason other than stress for her physical problems.

Now Marilyn watches her diet, has stopped smoking, gets plenty of rest, and jogs faithfully each day. She'd like someone to lean on occasionally and money pressures still upset her, but she's treating herself a lot better. She's eliminated many sources of stress in her life. No longer will she take a client on speculation. She checks out clients' credit ratings, she asks for money up front, or she'll do work COD. That relieved many of the money problems, but Marilyn learned the hard way how to pace herself.

Many women are under the mistaken belief that their hormones protect them from heart disease. That's one of the myths that has given women a false sense of security. Current research by the National Heart and Lung Institute shows that cardiac disease and hypertension are on the rise among women under the age of thirty-five. Women are also suffering from a higher incidence of ulcers and other gastro-intestinal (stress-related) diseases. The need to achieve outside of the household has contributed to a new set of female health problems.

So what's to be done about it? Most stress-management programs emphasize the development of a heightened sense of self-esteem.

Here are some practical suggestions. Keep physically fit; set aside fifteen minutes a day for exercise. Eliminate as many sources of stress from your life as you can. For example, while it is impossible to eliminate the weekly payroll, you can change a negative attitude toward paying your employees. Reflect on your

The Entrepreneurial Woman

deepest feelings concerning money. You probably feel a separation anxiety when you have to part with "your" money and give it to other people. You *can* change this attitude. Even if you need professional help to do so it's worth it, if only to reduce stress.

What other types of stress can you eliminate from your life? What about traffic and congestion? Move closer to work and save time in commuting. Does the noise in your place of business annoy you? Set aside a quiet area to work in. Are you overcommitted? Eliminate some extracurricular activities. Look at your calendar. Which days do you look forward to? Which ones would you like to avoid? Eliminate things that annoy you whenever possible and you'll be amazed at how much more relaxed you'll become.

Another way many entrepreneurial women handle stress is by talking about it. Find some friends who understand the pressures of businesswomen. Make them your confidantes and share the pains and pleasures of being in business. Talk about those lean periods. Talk about the pressures of your personal life and how they affect your business. Talk about learning to accept yourself as a business person. Form a support network.

Many people experience ups and downs as they get deeper and deeper into the problems and pleasures of running a business. The problem of selling capital assets to invest in business, the transition into thinking of yourself as a businesswoman, and the need to get your head in tune with what you're doing are all frightening experiences for the woman entering the world of business. No wonder her self-confidence may be shaky.

A close confidante was a necessity for one entrepreneurial woman who told me how she had sunk to an all-time emotional low. She didn't feel worthy as a businesswoman, a mother, or a human being. She'd been in business less than a year, had incorporated, and was overwhelmed by the amount of paperwork needed to keep up with state and federal laws. On top of this, she was a single parent with two children and was in the process of selling her house and moving to a smaller one. She had so many things going on at one time that she developed unbearable headaches. In addition, she had financial worries. She hadn't taken a salary from her business but had spent all her earnings on advertising, marketing, and operational expenses. She was a bundle of nerves, unable to eat or sleep. Fortunately she had a confidante who pulled her through those rough days.

I talked with her after the worst of her ordeal was over and she said, "I feel better now, and I know I'm going to make it. But for a while I was ready to give it all up."

A break in the routine also helps relieve stress. Carol Sumner-Appel, president of Sumner & Associates, a design firm in Los Angeles, takes mini-vacations throughout the year to take her away from her business pressures. She credits her house at the beach with helping her to survive the last five years of tremendous business growth. As she tells it, "I can *feel* my body posture change as I come off the freeway and head toward the beach. I avoid thinking about business for the entire weekend. It's a chance to get away from the city and the kids—if I choose—and put on my jeans and relax."

Mini-vacations are an excellent way to avoid the pressures that cause stress reactions in an overloading of the system.

BRAVE RESPONSES FOR SURVIVAL UNDER STRESS

Believe it or not, new ways of communicating can also help overcome stress. When we're under a great deal of stress, we may find ourselves locked into old behavior patterns that tend to reinforce our lack of self-esteem. Virginia Satir, a famous family therapist and consultant on interpersonal relations, has observed thousands of interactions between people afflicted with stress-related problems. She has found that there are basically four ways people respond to stress when their self-esteem is involved. She calls these communication patterns Brave Responses for Survival under Stress. These four patterns of communication are: blaming,

The Entrepreneurial Woman

placating, computing, and distracting.

In my communication and career-development workshops over the past six years, I have found Satir's model an excellent technique for helping women to become aware of their learned responses to stress. Once they are aware of these responses, they are often able to choose a more positive and appropriate response to stress.

A brief discussion of Satir's four communication patterns may help identify your own personal stress response. But remember, we're concerned with reactions to stress when your self-esteem is involved. There are times when stress is acute, but your self-esteem or self-worth are not in question. Then your response may be entirely different.

Do you know how you feel when your self-esteem is threatened? One entrepreneurial woman told this story. "I get butterflies in my stomach, my mouth gets dry, and I sometimes feel a lump in my throat. My face gets flushed, and I stumble over words. But I don't tell anyone how I feel. While these physical things are happening, I am engaging in an internal dialogue that sounds something like, 'They don't like me. Nobody cares about me. I'm in over my head. I can't do anything right.' People may see me at this time as anxious, overwrought, argumentative, embarrassed, or even incompetent. When I feel stress, I feel defensive and blame other people for my misfortunes. I'm tyrannical and become expert at cutting other people down."

Her brave response for survival under stress is patterned after Satir's blaming response. She feels negative about herself, and so feels that if she can blame someone else maybe she'll feel better. Usually it's a vicious cycle, and the person at the other end of her outburst becomes equally defensive and blames back.

Another woman with this blaming syndrome told me of the confrontations she used to have with her children and how these confrontations would escalate into small wars.

"I'd walk in the house, finger pointing, voice rising, yelling 'Why haven't you kids cleaned up around here? You never help out! You always expect your mother to be a slave!' and variations on that theme. The kids soon learned to fight back with 'You're the mother around here, you never bake us cookies, you never clean up your things, why should we help out!'"

Can you identify with this blaming response? Do you find yourself yelling at employees or suppliers, pointing the finger of blame at someone—anyone—for things that go wrong in the course of a business day? Or do you find yourself reacting to stress this way at home—thereby letting off the steam you fight to contain during the business hours? This type of behavior may cause migraine headaches, hypertension, or heart disease.

Barbara illustrated another one of Satir's responses—placating—when she told of a stressful situation with her banker.

"I have a hard time dealing with male chauvinism, especially when the people involved have power over me and my business. Things are definitely improving in the world for women in general, but the lending institutions are still in the Dark Ages in this area. I've tried several different banks in my eight years of business and unfortunately, most of the lending officers are male and old-fashioned to boot. One even laughed at my financial statement because it showed a savings account in the Feminist Federal Credit Union. Inside I was seething, but I kept a smile on my face as though his attitude didn't bother me. I knew I couldn't show my displeasure. He could turn down my loan. I acted simple, sweet, and helpless, because I knew that without his good will I would not get what I needed so badly. At some level, I denied all this to myself. It was as if I wasn't important enough, that I didn't count. He approved the loan, but I felt betrayed inside. I felt that he was glad to see me go and that even though I was so sweet and nice, he didn't really like me!"

Barbara was acting out Satir's placating response. She played the role of a martyr, and at some level the banker knew what was going on. That's probably why Barbara felt some hostility on his part. How do you feel at the other end of a placating martyr? Uncomfortable, I bet!

The Entrepreneurial Woman

"Acting like a machine" is what Satir calls the computing response. You think of yourself as a computer where the information comes in and the information goes out with no extraneous feeling involved. As humans, of course, we all have feelings. But the businesswoman whose survival techniques are those of the computer doesn't recognize feelings—hers or anyone else's! Feelings get in the way of expediency. Feelings get in the way of perfection. The "computer" doesn't recognize the lumpy feeling in her stomach until it's turned into an ulcer. She ignores the frequent tension and electricity in the air when employees aren't happy in their jobs and morale is low. She wants to deal only with the facts, with information. She is the entrepreneur who suddenly gets tension headaches, heart disease, backaches, a stiff neck and shoulders, and high blood pressure.

If computing is your brave response for survival under stress, you'll be ultrareasonable, calm, cool, and collected. You'll have all the numbers and figures at your command, and you'll be able to rely on experts and historical documentation to prove your point. Inside, however, you'll feel very shaky, and frightened of making a serious error. Sadly, many people hold the cool, calm, and collected business person as their model. We hear people say, "Isn't it marvelous, she never loses her composure." Well, she may *look* composed, but chances are she'll have some stress-related body ailment one of these days.

If you haven't found yourself yet in any one of these communications patterns, maybe you're the distractor. You may react to stress with the type of behavior that makes no sense to anyone around you. You may regress into a helpless little-girl role and talk baby talk. The distractor always jokes about adversity, never responds to the issue at hand. Her words are not to the point, and she ignores everyone's questions. People at the receiving end of her behavior feel disconcerted and confused.

Maybe she learned this response as a child. Perhaps when her parents or her brothers and sisters fought, she responded with a cute joke or a somersault. This always broke the tension then.

But it just won't work in business. You can't go around being irrelevant most of the time.

Since Satir calls these "brave" responses for survival, you may well ask what's so brave about them? The simple answer is that these responses are brave only on a superficial level. They can serve as coping mechanisms to help get you through the stress of the moment, but on a long-term basis, they will take their toll on you or on the people around you. So what can you do to develop authentic responses and not use these "brave" responses as the only means of survival?

Satir talks of a fifth response that she calls "leveling," or "flowing." This is the response that *is* authentic. By learning all the facets of the four stress responses and identifying which is your learned response for survival, you can begin to choose those that are appropriate. You can placate, blame, compute, or joke, with the difference being that you know what you're doing and *choose* to act in that way. You know what the consequences are and you're prepared for them.

In what situation might you choose to placate, and why would you want to? Picture a day in your junior boutique. You're having a sale, and the store is very crowded. One of your employees looks ready to come unglued. Three customers are vying for her attention while she's trying to write up a sale. You've been through those sales before and they don't get to you. You decide she needs help and you say, "Never mind about these customers, Sue, I'll take care of them. You look really overloaded, let me relieve you." What you've done is put yourself aside in favor of another whose need is greater. You're truly concerned about Sue, and at that time you choose to attend to her needs first. The difference between this and the learned placating response, however, is that you don't apologize for your actions in the process. Actually, this positive aspect of the placating response is called "affirming."

There are positive aspects to the blaming response, too. There are times in your business when you must criticize or

The Entrepreneurial Woman

evaluate a job that an employee or supplier is doing for you. The difference here is that you evaluate or criticize the job, or the act, NOT the person doing it. Remember—always separate the deed from the doer!

There also may be times in your business when you must explain details in a logical, orderly way. You must quote the experts to make your point. At times like these, you may feel a similarity to the computing response. The difference, however, is that you'll be moving freely, you'll be aware of your feelings and those of your audience, you'll invite questions and the sharing of information, and your entire presentation will be more open and inviting.

There may also be times when it's appropriate to reduce the tension. A sense of humor goes a long way as a part of the leveling response. The difference between tension reduction and irrelevancy is the timing and appropriateness of the response.

The whole difference between the brave response and the leveling response is that the latter is authentic. It represents the true feelings of a person in any given situation. The body, gestures, posture, and tone of voice are all consistent with the words being spoken.

If the above description seems similar to what you've read in earlier chapters about assertiveness training, you're making the right connection. That's why many stress-management classes put an emphasis on all aspects of assertiveness training, including the relaxation exercises. Satir's theory and assertiveness training have a lot in common. Both communication theories place a great value on heightened self-esteem.

Once you know who you are and can accept yourself, you'll be able to give yourself permission to relax, to assess the things in your life that are causing you stress, and to allow yourself the mini-vacations of the mind and/or body that can refuel you and help you deal with stressful situations. Accept yourself, be authentic. That is the best and most realistic method for coping with stress. Try it!

$$$$$$$$ **8** $$$$$$$$

Learning the hard way
• • •
things your lawyer or accountant never told you

*No business enterprise can succeed without sharing
the burden of the problem of other enterprises.*
—Ayn Rand

Just because you're not in the movies doesn't mean you won't see a casting couch.

Lots of women entrepreneurs have had to learn this the hard way—the same way they learned:

——Life isn't always fair.
——Friends and business don't always mix.
——Just because you've got a better mousetrap, the world will not necessarily beat a path to your door.
——All the world does not love a winner.
——It doesn't always pay to be patient.
——You can't do it all yourself.
——Don't take "No" for an answer.

If you believe in fairy tales with happy endings, most entrepreneurs will tell you to take a job in the local library. Many women business owners have learned the hard way that for every handsome prince you find, you run into a hundred ugly toads.

Take Lynn's case.

Lynn needed a security clearance to write proposals for government contractors. The government security agent had his hand on her knee and her blood pressure was rising. This is how Lynn tells it.

The Entrepreneurial Woman

"Since I'm still a woman in a male-dominated industry, I know a lot depends on my attitude. I'm serious about my work and most peple know it, but every now and then I run into problems. I don't have any trouble with suppliers or subcontractors, since they don't have any power over my business. But the government agent could have turned down my security clearance. I decided to ignore his leering glances, leading remarks, and hand on my knee. I think it bothered him more than if I had told him to stop doing it. Of course I had to grit my teeth to get through it, but I kept my cool. If I had to do it over again, I would have dressed more conservatively and acted icier.

"Another time, a loan officer suggested I take a trip to Palm Springs with him. He gave me the kind of look that said, 'Be nice to me and you'll get your loan.' I knew there were other banks in town, so I told him how I felt. He hasn't bothered me since, and he even approved the loan."

Every casting-couch situation is different, and there are no pat answers on how to handle them. What if you're hanging plants and notice that the men in the office can't take their eyes off your legs while you're on the ladder? What if you're installing plants in homes, and the customer greets you in his short robe? Or worse yet, what if you are trying to get a loan and your friendly banker becomes overly friendly? As we've seen, the variety of these instances can be endless.

There's no one way to respond to all these situations; you'll have to figure out each one for yourself. You can dress conservatively or you can invite the wolf home to meet your husband and children. You can also decide to be alert about whom you are dealing with, on which day, and for what purpose, and then costume yourself for the event. It's no fun to have to alter your dress and behavior because of some old-fashioned lecher, and it's certainly not fair that accepting a man's business dinner invitation might lead him to believe it's more than business—but whoever said life is fair? Coming up are some examples of just how unfair life can be.

LIFE ISN'T ALWAYS FAIR

Kay owned a marketing consulting firm with two male partners. She was invited to join the partnership for her administrative skills, but it soon became obvious that to advance in the partnership she would have to become a consultant. So she asked the senior partner to teach her the consulting end of the business. Since the business was growing, it made more sense to train her than to hire another consultant. In about three years, Kay had learned the marketing consulting very well—so well, in fact, that her mentor's clients often asked to see her.

Suddenly there was more and more administrative work to be done, and when Kay asked if she could hire an assistant, her partners said no. They decided to hire two junior (male) consultants to relieve Kay of her consulting "pressures" and free her for administrative busy work. Kay had bumped into male chauvinism but didn't catch on until it was too late. The partners were united in their stand and told her if she didn't like it, she could sell out. She found out life isn't fair!

There is a happy ending to this story, however. Kay is now in business for herself, without partners, and she's even taken a few clients away from her old firm.

Life didn't seem fair to Arlene either. Selling cars in a dealership, she felt the brunt of sex discrimination. Her employers made her feel like the "token woman," and she felt resistance from many customers. She thought she could escape this discrimination by going into business for herself, so she became a manufacturers' representative in the automotive after-market. She then learned that entrepreneurship was no ticket to a fair world. She tells it this way.

"A lot of the men I deal with think this field is too technical for a woman. That's ridiculous. Women are consumers, they earn money, and buy their own cars. Women also buy new tires, mufflers, and batteries for those cars and make decisions without a man's input. As a rep I can help my customers sell to women

The Entrepreneurial Woman

and get them into the store. It doesn't seem fair that my first year I had to work twice as hard as the male reps to be considered their equal. I had to make twice as many calls, and customers really put me through the hoops. They assumed that because a rep was male he knew everything about the product, so they threw a hundred technical questions at me every time I tried to sell them something. I've passed the test though, and now my customers accept me. They don't care who I am just as long as I deliver. I'm glad I stayed with it because I love the automotive business."

Fairness for women in male-dominated industries is rare, as the above stories illustrate, but Carla Sheridan's horror story about the fashion-importing business isn't much different.

When Carla went into the importing business, she was ahead of the game. Since this was her second go-around she'd already learned about import duties and how to get her goods through customs. But this time she had a mentor. Her story is fascinating.

"Everything seemed so perfect. Nick had been in retail men's clothing for years, importing high-quality apparel from Europe. Now his manufacturers were also making women's clothes and wanted him to carry their lines. He offered me the opportunity of a lifetime. He would introduce me to his suppliers and help me import a women's line. That way he could carry women's clothes in his store and not have to get involved with selecting and importing them—something he said he knew nothing about.

"It would be a chance for me to travel overseas and write off the trips as a business expense. And I'd have someone watching over me who spoke the language and knew his way around. Sounds like a perfect set up, right? *Wrong!*

"My mentor turned into my tormentor! I should have recognized it on our first trip to Greece. He treated me paternally, but I figured he had his reasons. If he wanted to think of me as a daughter, what difference did it make? I gritted my teeth and followed his advice on that first trip. I was in charge of picking out

Learning the hard way

the samples. At least he trusted my fashion sense. But when we got the samples back in the United States and I started selling the line to the carriage-trade stores in New York, Palm Beach, and Beverly Hills, he blew the whistle on me. He said, 'You can't sell clothes this way. The Italians and Greeks won't like it, they'll stop selling to you. I know these people and you don't—just trust me and it'll all work out fine!'

"Well, I believed him, and so I sold his way even though my intuition said it was wrong. The next year I went on a buying trip without Nick and talked to the manufacturers myself. I was amazed to find out that they weren't happy with the way I was representing them. They told me they had expected me to promote their lines just the way I had told Nick I wanted to. He'd given me a bum steer. Slowly it began to dawn on me—he didn't want me to succeed! He just wanted me to keep me around as his little dolly and show me off on his buying trips to Europe. I couldn't believe how naive I'd been. This kind of revelation is a real shocker when it finally happens

"When I started doing business my way, Nick really got angry. He threatened to ruin my reputation with my customers and the manufacturers in Europe. He called my showroom and antagonized my secretary. I began to think my phone was tapped, my business stationery disappeared, and then some manufacturers received letters from me which I hadn't written, canceling orders. It became clear that I had to drop my 'mentor.' I certainly learned the hard way from this experience; but it was 'precious knowledge dearly purchased.' And really, this kind of thing is enough to make anyone cynical."

None of these stories would surprise Vivien Kellums. Maybe she was onto something when she said, "Men always try to keep women out of business so they won't find out how much fun it really is."

So, where's the fun? Nancy had fun starting her business but after she had been in it a year she realized the validity of another truism:

JUST BECAUSE YOU'VE GOT A BETTER MOUSETRAP, THE WORLD WILL NOT NECESSARILY BEAT A PATH TO YOUR DOOR

Nancy is a business and financial consultant for women. When she started her business two years ago, she lectured, listed her name in directories, wrote letters to the editor, taught a financial-management class at the local junior college, joined professional associations, went to the meetings, and told everyone she met about her services. Business came in, and in a very short time she had more than she could handle. She received publicity through an article on the woman's page of the local paper, she was interviewed for a TV show, and her name was becoming a household word. She was so busy seeing clients that she began to turn down lectures, she had no time for interviews, and her brochure became dated. Her attendance at professional meetings lagged and she gave up teaching at the junior college. Well, wouldn't you know it—Nancy's business began to drag.

Nancy had let up on her marketing efforts. She began to believe her press clippings and thought people would beat a path to her door. She stopped hustling for business and became complacent because business was coming to her. She forgot that fame is fleeting at best. She'd been in business management for years, yet neglected her own advertising and marketing.

It's important to stay on top of your marketing efforts. Set aside time each week to review your business goals and fit your marketing plan to those goals. In a service business like Nancy's entrepreneurs recommend that you devote twenty-five percent of your time each week to business development.

Another mistake Nancy made was to rely on her friends for business and for word-of-mouth advertising. Her friends did support her at the beginning, but the discounts Nancy gave them never came back as new clients or referrals. Nancy found it cost her more to mix friendship with business than if she had offered her services to strangers at the very beginning. Which takes us to:

FRIENDS AND BUSINESS DON'T ALWAYS MIX

There are certain strategies you'll need to develop in dealing with the realities of the business world. One of the first is how to deal with your friends when they come to you for your business expertise.

If you have a service business, remember that the only thing you have to sell is your time. You are the product. Are you willing to sell yourself wholesale? Can you put a low price on your time and services?

When Patty became an interior decorator, she offered her services to her friends. After all, now that she had a resale number, the least she could do was to share her good fortune. She said, "If they only want to buy a lamp or something of that nature, I don't need to make any money on the deal. Then when they have a really big job to do, naturally they'll come to me." The myth of obligation was operating here, and after a few years of a losing business operation, Patty found out the following.

It costs just as much in time and energy to sell to a friend as it does to take a stranger on a shopping expedition through the furniture mart. In fact, there's probably a greater return when you're shopping with a stranger than when you're with a friend. "Every time I take a friend to the furniture mart or the design center, I get so annoyed with the way she wastes time. Shopping is a pastime for her. Doesn't she realize that shopping is my business and that my time is money?"

These are words spoken by the housewife being a decorator for her friends instead of a professional businesswoman. Which is it going to be for you? The key is to know yourself. What's more important to you—the love and approval of your friends, or a business run in a professional manner? Is your business only a labor of love, or are you also interested in profits?

Another aspect of mixing business with friendship involves taking a friend as a partner.

"Never again will I have a friend for a partner." Those words

The Entrepreneurial Woman

were spoken by at least ten entrepreneurial women interviewed. For these women, having a friend for a partner seemed like a good idea at the beginning, but their experience proved them wrong. The friendships are over, the partnerships disbanded, and many egos bruised in the process.

Before you start a business with a friend ask yourself if your friendship can survive the hard times. Have you had major disagreements and still maintained the friendship? A friend can give you courage and support, but in the long run it might be easier to join a support group or pay a therapist for this kind of help.

Tillie Johnson had a great idea for a business but was afraid to stick her neck out alone. She thought that if she had a partner, she'd have someone to commiserate with, brainstorm with, and work with. But what she found was that you can't always rely on a friend.

YOU CAN'T DO IT ALL YOURSELF

Tillie knew a lot about dolls, antique dolls in particular. She spotted a breakthrough in xerography that reproduced photographs on fabric, and her business idea was born. Almost Me Dolls was a booming mail-order business three months after it started, and Tillie couldn't handle it alone. This is how she tells the story.

"I got my idea to go into this business in the summer. I knew it would be successful because dolls with their owners' faces painted on oilcloth were something every little girl wanted at the turn of the century. I had to work fast to hit the market for Christmas orders so I spent my summer laying the groundwork. I lined up a loan, found subcontractors to make the pattern and sew the doll, found a fabric source, designed the clothes for the doll, and rented an office. I convinced a friend to join me in this venture, and I used my sister to set up our books.

Learning the hard way

"My idea was so good that after placing one ad we were overwhelmed by orders! Orders were coming in so fast that we worked ten-hour days, eight days a week! My partner wasn't prepared for the amount of time she would have to put into this business and so she left me holding the bag! I did the finishing, the shipping, the order-filling, the packaging, and the hiring of high-school students to help out. I was bringing dolls home for my kids to package. My house was filled with yarn hair. And my partner wasn't there! I was trying to do everything myself. I had a lot of courage and self-confidence, but what I didn't have was unlimited energy. My body just gave out on me. My thyroid began malfunctioning, and I was forced to sell the business one year after I had started it. One of the hardest things I learned was that I couldn't do everything myself!" This story has a happy ending. Tillie sold out at a handsome profit and regained her health.

While Tillie's success was a nightmare for her, many entrepreneurial women have discovered that instant success can hurt in other ways.

ALL THE WORLD DOES NOT LOVE A WINNER

Consider the story of Barbara and her cooking school. Hers was a case where instant success brought on jealous competition.

"I worked hard to start my cooking school, but I didn't talk about it to a lot of my friends before I actually opened for business. I spent time talking to the local food columnists and editors about my business ideas and what their readers were interested in. They were very willing to help me with suggestions and ideas, and with publicity. By the time I was ready to announce my opening I'd come up with some newsworthy items about my school and the courses I planned to offer.

"The Cuisinart food processor was just becoming popular, and so I developed a class called Cooking with Your Cuisinart. The title caught the fancy of the women's page editor, and so I

The Entrepreneurial Woman

received some free publicity. My classes filled right away, but I wasn't prepared for the reaction of some of my 'friends.' I guess they were hurt that I hadn't shared my ideas with them. They started offering cooking classes patterned after mine at the adult school, and they offered them free, since the school district paid for the classes. I was really angry. That was certainly an introduction into the world of business! I know competition is a reality—but from your friends?"

Like all entrepreneurs, Barbara realized she would have to come to grips with competition. She created other ideas to attract students, and eventually people recognized the quality of her classes. She publicized the fact that her classes were small and personalized, and she offered a unique service in her school. She sold fancy cookware to her students at special prices, something the adult school couldn't do. She found her school could be successful even in the face of competition.

Competition is just one aspect of the "all the world doesn't love a winner" syndrome. Lots of entrepreneurial women have reported that a winning track record doesn't always impress the local officers at banks either. Here's a story from one woman on that subject.

"I'd been in business for almost two years and had grown to the point where I had a cash-flow problem. I needed about $50,000 to get me over the hurdle, and I had more than $200,000 in accounts receivable to back it up. Well, the bank wouldn't give me accounts-receivable financing. It wanted my husband to co-sign the loan, using our house as collateral! I felt the bank should have treated me the same as any businessman applying for a loan, as my business credentials were very good. Finally, though, I just gave in and let my husband co-sign the loan. The same thing happened with my landlord—he made me get my husband to co-sign my lease. His reason was that this is a community property state, although I never remember co-signing for my husband's business interests.

"I think both the banker and the landlord are breaking laws

Learning the hard way

by not treating women equally, but I didn't have the energy to fight it. I know I didn't have to take 'No' for an answer, but I did. I just turned the other cheek and let my husband come to my rescue."

Turning the other cheek may work in some business situations, but consider Jan's story.

DON'T TAKE "NO" FOR AN ANSWER

"I run a computer software business and lost out on a job project recently. I put so much time into developing my proposal that it never occurred to me I wouldn't get the job. I was bidding against two firms that didn't have as good a track record as my firm, so I thought I had it made. When I didn't get the job I decided to find out why. I phoned the buyer and asked if I could meet with him. I said I'd like his help so that I might get better results next time. He sounded nervous at my request, but agreed to see me the following week.

"When I showed up for our appointment, I was surprised to see that he had included his boss in the meeting. It was obvious that he expected trouble. As we talked, I tried to set them at ease, but they were overly prepared with facts about why the other firm got the job. I put two and two together and realized that the buyer was a government contractor with an obligation to buy from women and minority-owned firms. The successful bidder was a white, male-owned firm that was probably connected through a brother-in-law to the company. When I saw what was going on, I laughed and decided that there was probably going to be more business available from this company and so it would be best to leave the two men feeling that I respected them and wanted their business. My goal for that meeting was to seek their help and advice to make that happen. It worked too. Even though I didn't get the big job I originally went after, I now have several small assignments for next year. I guess the key here was my attitude. I

The Entrepreneurial Woman

would not accept rejection as personal, and I wanted to learn from it."

Jan learned that even though you're in business for yourself, you can't always escape the politics and realities of "let's give the business to my brother-in-law." But she made it work for her and didn't take "No" for an answer. She also learned to break through the phone barriers and deal with rejection.

There are various kinds of phone barriers, and you need to know about them. Just because your service or product is the "hottest thing in town," doesn't mean that everyone will want to talk to you. How will you deal with getting through the secretaries to the person in charge? What will you do if everyone you call is "in a meeting" or has "just stepped out for a moment"? And what if a day goes by and no one calls you back? Will you take the rejection personally?

A letter preceding the phone call might help. Or you might simply try calling again until your call is returned. Some salespeople have confessed to making as many as ten calls before getting to talk to the right person. Listen to how Leah tells it.

"I cringe when I have to keep calling someone who hasn't returned my call. I feel as though I'm a pest and that no one wants to buy my product. But, so many times, when I've finally gotten through (usually because the secretary is embarrassed by then), I've managed to get an appointment and I've even sold some large orders that way. But it's hard, and I have to keep plugging. I know if I waited for them to call back I might never get to anyone. In this business, where sales are so important, it doesn't pay to be patient."

IT DOESN'T ALWAYS PAY TO BE PATIENT

Jessica, the owner of a junior sportswear chain, also found that it doesn't pay to be patient. Her business is successful, but that didn't impress the contractors she hired to redo her stores.

Learning the hard way

"Some contractors tend to take advantage of you if you're a woman," Jessica told me. "I found this out the hard way. After remodeling four stores it suddenly dawned on me that not everyone had my kind of problems with carpenters, painters, and plumbers. I'd make plans for them to get started on a job and it would be days before they'd show up. But whenever my husband called and got tough with them, they'd show up the next day. I got tired of relying on my husband to play the bad guy, and since it is my business, I decided to take matters into my own hands. This is what I do now: I insist on a written bid for each job, outlining exactly what is to be done, who is to do it, who will supervise the job, what it will cost, and what is the expected date of completion. I also insist on a penalty clause if the completion date goes over their estimate by thirty days. I've found this keeps the contractors on their toes.

"I even sued one of the men for breach of contract. Since it's a small world out there and these men talk to one another, I get better service now.

"The worst thing you can do is be patient! I used to believe them when they said they'd be on the job 'tomorrow.' I kept waiting for the tomorrows, believing that people were basically good and wouldn't deliberately lie. Well, I was wrong. Some people would rather humor you and tell you they'll be there than tell you the truth and disappoint you up front."

Lila also learned the hard way that it doesn't pay to be patient. She had three kids to support, no husband, and no money when she took a job in an employment agency in exchange for the promise of future equity in the business. He employer paid her a low salary and commission, just enough to get by on. Her kids shared one bedroom and she slept in the living room.

She was patient, waiting for the business to get to the point where she would be made a partner and reap the rewards. A year went by and then another, and although business was growing, there were still the excuses that it wasn't profitable enough for her to be taken on as a partner.

The Entrepreneurial Woman

Lila recognized that without her and her clients the business would be nothing at all, and that she deserved a partnership. As there was still obviously no partnership in store for her, she quit.

Because of her experience, her list of temporary employees, and her client contacts, Lila was able to get a small loan and start her own employment agency. She had the good sense to get out of the trap her patience had gotten her into.

Another patience trap to avoid is letting your accounts receivable become too long overdue. There's no way you can afford to be patient when people owe you money. But, as many entrepreneurs have reported, it's not always easy to spot a deadbeat, and sometimes patience is preferable because it's unpleasant to be demanding.

"Asking for money is the worst part of my business. I wish I was successful enough to hire someone else to handle the accounts receivable." These are words spoken by many entrepreneurial women. One woman, however, had an enlightening story to tell about how she's learned the collection trick.

"Whenever a customer pays me," she says, "I write down the name and branch of his or her bank in my books. This way, if I have any trouble with that client later, I always know where the money is. I sell plants and install them in offices, and some of my clients are so 'successful' that they can't be bothered with small bills like mine. One high-priced accountant kept ignoring my bills, so I decided to take him to small claims court. I had him served in his fancy office, and he called me immediately saying he'd pay the bill. I found out that it really isn't so difficult to take someone to small claims court, and usually the process server will be just enough of a scare to get the bill paid. I also make customers pay the costs I've incurred in collection."

By now, you've probably figured out that businessmen (and businesswomen) seem to play a tremendous number of games. How do you cope with these games? How can you win, or at least see that you don't lose? Do you have to learn the hard way? Not necessarily, but you have to stay alert.

Learning the hard way

Watch out for these common business "games."

—**"The Check's in the Mail."** Maybe it is and maybe it isn't, but don't extend any more credit until the check has cleared the bank.

—**"It's Thirty Percent Less Across the Street."** If you can't match your competitor's price and still achieve your margin goals, don't. You're in business to make money. Remember the classic butcher story about the customer who told the butcher that the T-bone steaks were a dollar a pound less across the street. The butcher told the customer to buy them across the street, to which she answered that the butcher across the street was all out of T-bones. He said, "Mine are also a dollar a pound less when I'm out of them."

—**"Don't Trouble Your Pretty Little Head."** The worst kind of patronizing! *Do* trouble your head. Don't get involved in deals that you don't fully understand. Learn before you get burned—the fine print can hurt.

—**"Have I Got a Deal For You!"** Don't believe in tall tales. If a total stranger makes you an offer you can't refuse, make sure you understand why. Look for the catch before you get caught in this game.

—**"It's Our Company Policy."** Policies are designed to eliminate the need for thinking and questioning. Don't ever be afraid to question policy. A variation of this game is "But This is the Way We've Done It for Years." It's just an excuse for not changing.

—**"Trust Me, It's the Hottest Thing in Town."** This game is usually played by dropping a lot of big names: "Bonwits bought the whole line," or "Xerox says it's the newest thing in the computer industry," or "Liza Minelli and Barbra Streisand buy directly from this designer." When you hear this game, think of a dance—the Hustle—and sit it out.

The Entrepreneurial Woman

——**"I'm Just a Country Boy."** Shucks, if you fall for this game of tricking you into revealing your proprietary methods, you deserve to be taken. Don't ever underestimate the intelligence or cunning of your customers.

——**"This Is on the Back Burner."** Sometimes you'll get a contract in six months, sometimes you won't. You may be dealing with a gamester who doesn't feel comfortable saying "No."

The challenge of game playing is fun, especially when you get past "go," but in business, as in Monopoly, strategy and knowledge of the game help. It's more than a toss of the dice that will decide whether or not you end up owning all the railroads and Park Place.

Sometimes we forget to follow our instincts; we get caught up in a game, and find ourselves in trouble. Well, don't be too hard on yourself. Just learn from the experience so that you can come out ahead the next time.

Remember the game Snakes and Ladders? Well, business can be like that. One day you can be in the "pits" with the snakes and next day climbing the ladder to business success.

The next chapter will deal with the practical steps involved in climbing that ladder.

$$$$$$$$ 9 $$$$$$$
Starting your own business

Creative planning and creative unplanning are both essential.
—Holly Harp

You've come far enough in this book to know that running your own business may not measure up to your fantasies of glamour, freedom, riches, and fame. You know it's going to include hard work, long hours, and a good deal of stress. But, you want to do it anyway. So now comes the vital question—how will you get your business off the ground?

The experts, the MBA's and the SBA's, will tell you to sit down and very carefully define your business, your objectives, your marketing approach, and summarize your estimates of expected sales, profits, and capital required. You're supposed to add a twenty-five percent to fifty percent contingency, anticipate your time schedule for opening, allow for inflation, deflation, recession, war, poverty, death and famine, and ultimately draw up a trial P & L (Profit and Loss) statement and balance sheet for the first two years by months. Then you are advised to make a cash-flow analysis for two years, a break-even chart for minimum sales, and a fixed-asset acquisition schedule by month. When you have finished preparing this financial statement, you're then supposed to know whether or not it makes sense to start the business.

Many entrepreneurial women, on the other hand, will offer an opposing argument to all this preparation. They'll tell you that at first they thought P & L meant "payments and loans" and that a financial statement was something you get from a bank.

The Entrepreneurial Woman

A number of extremely successful entrepreneurs found that the requirements for setting up a business were intimidating and even overwhelming, but they went into business anyway. They didn't let the experts' advice slow them down. They had ideas on how to make money. They planted a few seeds, cultivated and tilled, added plenty of good fertilizer, and found their businesses growing profusely. Few of the women interviewed for this book started with any formal, detailed business plan. Many started their businesses with the help of their own intuition and have created ventures that are profitable and growing.

Charisma and a hustler's personality have carried many small businesses through the first few years. Eventually, however, most entrepreneurs discover the need for establishing goals and doing financial planning in order to make the business grow. But in the beginning, many just went into business!

Should you develop a business plan? It's hard to take a firm stand against the virtues of good, solid planning. How can you argue against taking a long, hard look before you leap? The problem is that most of the advice and counsel that you will get in preparing a business plan is likely to be overly complicated, filled with confusing business jargon, and thoroughly frightening.

Here's what I believe. Yes, you should plan. You should have an idea of how much your business will cost, how much you can take in, and what your financial needs will be. BUT—you don't have to know how to write a Harvard School of Business document to do it. As a matter of fact, you shouldn't let the need for making a business plan immobilize or intimidate you and keep you from opening the business of your dreams.

If you need help from a lending institution, if you want to start a major enterprise with several employees, or a large factory with significant capital equipment, the question is academic. You absolutely will need a business plan. Help is available from the library on how to write a business proposal. Financial institutions are also a good source of information. For example, the Bank of America offers a series of booklets, *The Small Business Reporter*,

Starting your own business

on subjects such as understanding financial statements, financing small businesses, steps to starting a business, advertising, and cash flow. Write to *The Small Business Reporter*, Bank of America, Department 3120, P.O. Box 37000, San Francisco, CA 94137. Postage and handling charges are $1.00 per copy.

If you still can't bring yourself to write your proposal, try to locate a business development consultant who can help you. This consultant may be a lawyer, accountant, or banker. It may be a person like Beatrice A. Fitzpatrick of the American Women's Economic Development Corporation in New York, or Nancy Mills of Ms. Management in Los Angeles.

Ms. Management is a business development service offering practical planning, guidance, and consultation for women starting their own businesses. Nancy Mills works individually and in groups with potential entrepreneurial women, helping them to focus and write their business plans.

Nancy says: "The name of the game in business is planning, and planning can decrease the fears women have about going into business. I think writing a business plan is a process which helps a woman focus on her goals and profit potential. There's no reason to be in business unless you're in business to make a profit."

Whatever you do, make sure the consultant is on your wavelength and that you're taken seriously as a businesswoman. Remember, you're buying a service, so select someone who is knowledgeable and experienced in your type of business. It may take you several months or more to put your business plan together, so choose someone you respect and with whom you will enjoy working.

In this chapter we'll touch on a few ventures that grew almost accidentally, without a business plan, and we'll detail one that was carefully planned.

A Cincinnati, Ohio woman with great charisma and style tells about her business this way.

"I started selling sample clothes that a few of my salesmen

The Entrepreneurial Woman

friends had left over at the end of the season. I racked them up in my basement and invited some friends over to look through them and possibly buy. They brought their friends along. More salesmen left me their clothes, and pretty soon I had more than I could handle from my basement. One of my friends told me about a store I could rent for a few dollars. I said, 'Why not?' and before I knew it, I had a fairly large business. That was ten years ago. Today, my store is 2,000 square feet, I employ seven saleswomen, and I go to the annual markets. I'm in business!"

Here are two other stories about entrepreneurial women who were able to make their businesses grow and succeed with very little up-front planning.

Norma Saken's story goes like this.

"I was divorced and couldn't do anything but cook. My girlfriend and I decided to go into the catering business. She knew a single man who was the head of catering for a large hotel in town, and she figured she could kill two birds with one stone if she introduced me to him. I cooked a fine dinner for him and he was so impressed with it, and with us, that he helped us get started by referring us to our first customers.

"We called our business Saycheese, and our first clients were executives at ABC television. We offered only elegant gourmet fare and charged from twenty-five to fifty dollars per person, so we were assured of a fairly large profit margin. I'd been a waitress for a while, so I was able to use my contacts and hire other waitresses and bartenders to work for us. Our strong points were that we were great cooks, and we were personable and attractive. I was raised to be a hostess, and I didn't find catering so different from being married.

"We had a very impressive group of clients. We served the 'kings of industry and government' at our luncheons—one time, even the governor of California. From ABC we went to Paramount. The business was one of those things that just evolved. But let me tell you, the work was grueling, the hours were long, and it didn't leave much time for a social life."

Starting your own business

You'll read more about Norma in Chapter 11, but here's Valerie's story.

"I had worked as a decorator for two firms before I started my own. I began my business without a plan, but I did have a client who was furnishing a large home, and those commissions could support me for a while. I had some money from my divorce settlement to get purchase orders, business stationery, office supplies, and a telephone. Since I ran my business from my home, I didn't need a lot of money to get started.

"When I didn't know how to do something I asked for help or got advice. I needed to keep good books and records, but organization and management weren't my strong points, so I hired a great organizer and bookkeeper. My business grew. Since it's a service business operating with clients' money, as long as I keep getting clients and serving them well, we'll stay in business. I still don't have a plan detailing long-range goals, but I do know where I've been. It's five years since I started, and I now have a large office with five employees, I meet a regular payroll, have learned to read financial statements, and can meet intelligently with my accountant to go over my records. Believe me, when the numbers are yours, you know what they mean."

Unusual stories? Not at all. Women have started all kinds of enterprises in a similar manner: fashion and design studios, consulting businesses, importing companies, employment agencies, toy stores, restaurants, diet salons, nursery schools, dance studios, and even paper-hanging services. They've started businesses in garages, lofts, basements, spare rooms, laundry rooms and high-rises. One entrepreneur I interviewed ran the business from her car and from pay phones as she drove along. If you've got an idea and the determination to see it through, the lack of business experience, a business plan, or a business manager won't stop you.

You don't have to wait *until*—*until* you figure out how to write the business plan, *until* you get the courage to approach an accountant or lawyer with your idea—the "untils" may never

The Entrepreneurial Woman

happen. You'll know when you need a business plan—so get moving! One day you'll wonder "Am I, in fact, making any money from this business?" or "Can I afford to expand the business?" That's when you'll write your plan.

The factor that the business experts cannot take into account is your own individual personality—your determination to succeed, your refusal to even consider the possibility of failure. So many women entrepreneurs have said, "I never gave failure a chance. If I made a mistake, I learned something valuable for the next time. I just picked up the pieces and kept on going." Along with a good business idea, that's the attitude you'll need for success.

You can start small and learn the "ins and outs" of business as you go along. It's done all the time, and sometimes with amazing results. One very successful manufacturer knew she was on her way to success when she had to trade her shoe boxes for a file cabinet. She started out keeping records on the calendar in her kitchen and paying her suppliers from the family checkbook. She was in business for almost a year before she saw the need for a business bank account, systems, and a total business plan. The point is that for a certain period of time your own native intelligence, good judgment, and sound intuition can carry you through. You'll know when it's time to put your plans down on paper or ask for help.

Some businesses, on the other hand, require detailed planning and preparation right from the start. Karen Russo's and Carol Landolfi's Discovery Travel in Redondo Beach, California is one such business. Because it is a travel agency, they needed heavy bonding and accreditation from the Air Traffic Conference (ATC) and International Air Transport Association (IATA). Karen and Carol opened their business recently, so the steps they took in planning are still fresh in their minds. Karen describes it.

"We knew we wanted to go into business together. We had both worked in the same travel agency, got along well, and wanted to be on our own. We kicked the idea around an

Starting your own business

checked out the existing travel businesses that were up for sale. We talked to owners of other travel agencies, gathering information about the laws and regulations affecting the business. You wouldn't believe the faulty information we got from people trying to 'help' us. Because the regulations keep changing in this industry, the best place to get information, we found, was directly from the source. We saved a lot of time and money when we finally contacted the ATC in Washington, D.C.

"Carol and I started talking seriously about opening our own travel agency in February, when we concluded that it would cost four times as much to buy an existing travel agency as it would to open our own. Also, we didn't want to be stuck with the other agency's image and troubles. We wanted to build a new image and take advantage of our own creativity.

"We both had travel plans for February and March. Carol was going to the Orient in March, and I was going to Alaska in February. Before I left, we researched sites and decided to locate within a certain ten-mile area in a beach city. Nothing was available before I left, so we decided to table our plans until I returned.

"When I came back, I noticed a choice storefront vacant in Redondo Beach, although there was no 'For Rent' sign on it. We watched it for days, and still no sign. Meanwhile, Carol left for the Orient. She'd been gone three days when the 'For Rent' sign went up. I wired Carol in Hong Kong and signed the lease two days later. This was my first experience in negotiating a lease. I was so excited about finding the right location that I would have given almost anything to get the lease, but my husband slowed me down. He negotiates leases as a part of his work, and he showed me how to bargain for interior improvements as part of our lease. That was my first lesson. There were to be many more during those first few weeks. We didn't just sign the lease and open our doors to the world. We had lots more to do.

"We had to figure out how to get ATC and IATA appointments, how to get bonding, and how to set up the legal structure

The Entrepreneurial Woman

of the business. We had to furnish and decorate the place, get stationery, business forms, and set up accounting systems. There were days when I wondered if we would ever open for business because of all the detail work.

"We found that we needed to develop our own group of experts to help us plow through the details. We asked almost everyone we knew for advice. One travel agent offered to act as our consultant in getting an ATC appointment for a mere $5,000! That would have been a waste of money, as we found that it's quite easy to pick up the phone and call the ATC in Washington yourself. Somebody told us that ATC and IATA only meet twice a year. We found that they both review applications monthly and that it usually takes from forty-five to ninety days for approval. That part was easy, but there was a *Catch 22* situation that gave us some problems.

"The catch is that you can't get ATC and IATA appointments unless you're already set up for business, and without the appointments, you can't get ticket stock. So what do you do? You take ticket orders from your clients and then you run to the airport and buy the tickets at the airline ticket counter. You stand in line just like a tourist—this must be the first test of your determination.

"On top of that, you have to prove to the ATC and IATA that you are really in business. You do that with a proposal that ends up the size of a small telephone book. It includes your business stationery, recommendations from upstanding citizens, your IRS number, business license, logo, and a picture of your office and sign. It also documents the two years' previous travel agency experience you must have to meet their requirements.

"Then, they check out your financial stability and send a representative to investigate you and your business personally. The worst part is that you never know when they're going to make their inspection, so even though you don't have ticket stock, you've got to actually be in business. We took no lunches for two months, waiting for the inspector to come.

"My sister, who is a student in graphic design, did our logo

Starting your own business

and got our stationery business forms printed up. That was a definite help since it enabled us to get all our materials for the application together in about a month.

"It seemed as though there were thousands more things to do, however, and we worried that it would all fall apart at any minute. The worst part involved trying to get our bonding. Travel agencies need a minimum $10,000 bond because of all the negotiable blank tickets they hold. We found a bonding company that we thought would do the job for us. They were about fifty miles away on the other side of Los Angeles County. We drove there, presented our credentials, outlined our experience, showed our business plan, and got turned down flat! The man said, 'Women don't have a high rate of success in business, and you gals don't have any business experience.'

"You can imagine how we felt about that snap judgment. After a combined eight years of experience in the travel business, he tells us we don't have any business experience! Once again my husband came to the rescue. He called the bonding agent, described our financial and personal stability, and convinced him to sell us the bond. Prejudice against women seems to be a fact of life, but I still can't accept it. It makes me very angry."

Did Karen and Carol also write up a business plan? Yes.

Karen goes on to say, "As our business was financed with personal funds, we didn't have to apply for a loan, but we worked out a business plan anyway. It was our money, and we wanted to make sure we were setting down goals in order to turn a profit. And it now looks like we're on the right track because we've exceeded our first four-month projection at the end of two and a half months! We decided to set up the business as a general partnership instead of a corporation. The airlines prefer it that way initially so they can hold us personally liable for any defaults. An attorney friend helped us draw up the partnership agreement, and my husband's expertise was useful in setting up our accounting system.

"Six weeks after we opened, we had a grand-opening party

The Entrepreneurial Woman

that brought us some good client leads. But nothing we did at first was commissionable until we had the ATC appointment.

"Was I ever happy when that came! We've finally got our own ticket stock. Now we're waiting to hear from IATA. I called their office in Montreal and found out that we can expect their approval at any time. ATC's approval was the most crucial though, since most of our business is domestic.

"Our capital expenditures included our office furniture, display racks for travel brochures, phone installation, stationery, a sign, and money for utilities and incidental supplies. We also budgeted for a trip to Washington, D.C., as part of our start-up expenses because we decided we'd get our appointment faster from the ATC if we presented our application in person. It worked, too. Ours was a record time for an appointment.

"It's helped to have customers from our former agency—both of us had developed a following over the years. Our former boss has been terrific and wrote us an extraordinary letter of recommendation, which was very important in getting our approval from the airlines.

"Neither of us has taken a salary yet, as all our money goes to pay for tickets and overhead. Now that we have our ticket stock, we'll be able to collect our back commissions and we won't have to go to the airport every day.

"Now that we have our tickets we're going to start our marketing effort in earnest. We have a marketing program prepared, and we plan to go after commercial business, since we both have executive contacts. We understand the special accommodations necessary for traveling executives, and we plan to create a specialized service for them. We understand our clientele since we've had several years of experience dealing with such people. We also plan to provide customized travel experiences, using our imagination and creativity to offer unique travel packages. We've put together chartered yacht trips and now we're considering a businesswomen's guided tour to the trade fair in China. Things like this make the business worthwhile.

Starting your own business

"We've learned to use all our contacts. My husband, with his business expertise, has provided the greatest help, though it wasn't easy to admit how much we rely on him. For example, the hardest part for Carol and me is keeping the books. But the need for good record keeping is basic, and we have to understand our system before we can delegate it. Once again, thank heavens for my husband—he's helping us out at the beginning with the books and he's teaching us as he goes along. He also used his contacts to help us buy furniture and other office supplies. Let's face it, resources from a big business can buy at a better rate than two women just starting out."

Halfway through our interview, Karen's husband, who was on his lunch hour, arrived to go over the books. How times have changed! In the past the wife helped out in the business, and the husband ran the show! Karen has learned to trust John's financial ability, and both she and Carol know they have a lot to learn about financial matters. Of course they're not alone. Many small-business owners don't know a thing about financial statements and cost-control systems.

I could sense it wasn't easy for Karen to let her husband take over the books, and I asked her how she handles this. "I lose my temper when John criticizes the way I've made entries in the books," she said, "but I'm just learning. Underneath it all, I know we're in business for a profit, and he wants us to succeed. It's just hard handling the personal and emotional side of it. Carol and I want to do it ourselves, and eventually we will. But for now, we need John's expertise and we're grateful to have it."

Most new businesses can't afford to hire a business manager to take over daily operations, but a lot of free help is available if you look for it. Even if you don't have a husband to pitch in and help out, consider looking for a retired business executive to help you put your books together or give you other business advice. Contact your local Small Business Administration office, listed in the phone book under U.S. Government. To help you, the SBA has a task force of volunteers called SCORE (Service Corps of

The Entrepreneurial Woman

Retired Executives). If you're lucky you'll get a SCORE volunteer who will understand your business needs and can work with you. On the other hand, you might get a retired insurance executive who is eager to help you in setting up your interior decorating business but doesn't know the slightest thing about it, or you might get one who thinks women belong in the home. Keep trying, be persistent! Just because one SCORE volunteer doesn't work out, that doesn't mean that another one won't be able to help you. Remember, most are senior citizens and things have changed drastically in the business world. They may not be used to assertive women running their own enterprises.

Some SCORE volunteers get a vicarious thrill out of watching "their" businesses succeed. And if it's to your benefit to put your "politics" aside for your enterprise's sake and allow an old-fashioned man to treat you like yesterday's woman, then do it! Remember, you don't have to follow all of his advice—you're still in charge.

An importer I know in Santa Barbara developed a very close friendship with a SCORE volunteer. He had been in the importing business and was able to share his expertise with her. He helped her thread her way through the import laws, saved her from many pitfalls, and even gave her some sales training in the process.

But let's get back to Karen and Carol so we can examine the steps they took as they started their business.

First of all, it's important to look at their personal characteristics, relating back to Chapter One.

Both of them fit the model of displacement. Their children are now teenagers and don't require their constant availability. Carol's recent divorce emphasized her need for more money.

They're both very achievement-oriented and independent. They had experience in the travel business, and both had traveled extensively. They had the resources to start their own business, both in terms of finances and energy. Their families supported their idea and were willing to make some sacrifices at home.

The Small Business Administration offers a pamphlet,

Starting your own business

Checklist for Going into Business, which takes you through the steps of opening an enterprise. It's available from your local SBA office (there are more than ninety-one offices nationally, with at least one in every state). Ask for *SMA (Small Marketers Aids) 71*.

Karen and Carol met the requirements of the SBA's basics before they opened their doors. These basics included:

—Personal Data. They both had the entrepreneurial characteristics as outlined in Chapter One and in the SBA checklist. They were also committed to spending long hours and weeks running their business. They both had experience in the travel business and were willing to be not only travel agents but clerk, secretary, messenger, and janitor as well.

—Money Data. They projected how much money would be needed to set up the business and how much they needed to live on. They also sought advice for setting up their books and projecting their cash flow. They agreed on and wrote up a business plan. They prepared a financial statement as part of the business plan.

—Form of Business. They agreed on a partnership and formalized their agreement with the help of an attorney.

—Source of Customers. Issues such as the kinds of people who would buy their services influenced their choice of location. They also knew they had a following from their previous job, so they could count on an immediate source of business.

—Site Location. They looked into more than just the neighborhood. They considered competition and other businesses in the area, the amount of foot traffic, parking and zoning requirements. They negotiated a long-term lease and had improvements made in the facility.

—Equipment and Supplies. They made a list of what they needed, keeping in mind the image they wanted to project. They knew that business forms were necessary from their previous

The Entrepreneurial Woman

experience. They were able to buy their furniture and office equipment at a better rate, using Karen's husband's contact.

—What to Sell. That's pretty cut-and-dried in this business, but they researched new resources for travel packages and also investigated the new airline rates and services available.

—Record Keeping. They devised a record-keeping system to keep track of accounts payable and receivable. A weekly reporting system was set up for reporting ticket sales to the airlines.

—Business and the Law. They bought the necessary licenses and researched the laws and regulations that governed their business. They talked to a lawyer and established a relationship for ongoing advice.

—Protection. They got an insurance bond for the tickets and an office safe and a safe-deposit box for their ticket stock. They also purchased a liability policy, which was a requirement of their lease. The office also has an alarm system.

—To Start a Business or Buy an Existing One? They researched both aspects and found that it was more economical in this case to start their own business.

Now that Karen and Carol are in business, they've also devised detailed plans for making it work. These points are also covered in the SBA pamphlet and they include:

—Advertising. The first phase of their advertising and promotional campaign was a grand-opening party. They sent invitations to everyone they knew, old customers and friends alike. Many people who didn't know they were in business have now become customers, so the party was a success. Now that they have an ATC appointment, they're beginning to advertise in the local papers and will continue with a direct-mail campaign to business contacts. They have a marketing plan that they are following. There's a budget for the first year's advertising and promotion.

Starting your own business

—Price to Charge. In this business, pricing is pretty much regulated by the airlines and the hotels. But Carol and Karen have decided to offer their customers extra value by providing a personal touch. For instance, Karen meets with couples in the evenings in their homes to help plan vacations, even advising clients on the appropriate wardrobe for their trip. Since both owners have traveled widely themselves, they are able to share more than scheduling and ticketing expertise with their clients.

—Buying. Most retail businesses have inventory to consider. This is not a large consideration in the travel business. However, Carol and Karen must keep up their supply of tickets, and since the airlines have a three-week lead time for ordering, the two women must be accurate in their projections of ticket stock to meet their needs. They also need to stay current with the travel brochures and rate schedules provided by the airlines and large tour packages. These are automatically sent to travel agencies once, but reorders are the responsibility of the travel agents.

—Sales Techniques. Carol and Karen know what sells in their community. They've established a quality image by their location, decor, and visual materials. They're both outgoing, personable types, willing to go the extra steps to provide special services for their customers. They count on repeat business, and they're getting it. They follow up on all inquiries, calling potential customers with requested information, even if the person has no immediate travel plans. They know that when the time comes for travel, tickets will be booked through their business. Their future sales plans include community contact to develop a market for group tours, lectures, and travelogues.

—Employees. Future plans include hiring clerical help, more agents, and eventually opening a branch, but for now, it will be just the two of them.

—Credit. They researched bank credit cards and discovered it was best to write tickets using national credit services. That way

The Entrepreneurial Woman

it's an automatic transaction, billed by the airlines to the credit services. All fees must be paid when they hand over the tickets. Airline regulations guide them as to whether or not to give credit to customers. Deposits are always collected before hotel accommodations are booked, and they accept checks only from customers with whom they've done previous business.

Karen and Carol have also built into their business plans a contingency for the unexpected. They estimated their operating costs for the first year and doubled them. This allows for any unforeseen costs that may arise. They haven't had to dip into their "excess fund" yet, but it's comforting to know it's there.

The owners of Discovery Travel seem to have prepared themselves for success. They haven't let the dismal statistics of small-business failures get in their way. They know that according to Dun & Bradstreet about fifty-five percent of all new businesses fail by the end of five years, but they also know that this number includes businesses that have failed because of incompetence, inexperience, and because of individuals who were not prepared for the realities of business.

Do the planning and research they put into their business seem like too much for you? Don't let it stop you. Get moving—you can do it!

$$$$$$$$ **10** $$$$$$$$

That first sale... I didn't even know what to charge

*If you clearly visualize yourself making good—
very good—money
all your efforts will be concentrated on making it happen.*

This chapter tells you all about M-O-N-E-Y. It's about the wonderful energizing effects of money, the mysticism surrounding how much to charge, and some tips from entrepreneurial women on how to get your fair share of it.

It takes a long time for some women to stop thinking in terms of small change and to believe that they are worth the price they're asking for their goods and services. Again, it's those old feelings about money and women in society. Let's get the platitudes out of the way.

Which ones do you remember from earlier days:

—Money is the root of all evil.

—Money doesn't grow on trees.

—Money talks.

—Money is power.

—Money attracts money.

—Money, men earn it, women spend it.

—Money determines value in our society.

—Money, you get what you pay for.

—Money, it's better to give than to receive.

No wonder it's so hard to think straight about money!

The Entrepreneurial Woman

Sumie Mishima, a designer with her own company, Visual Resources, Inc., specializing in film and graphics, credits much of her success to an ability to candidly discuss money. She worked for design studios and advertising agencies before forming her own firm, and so became accustomed to quoting substantial fees. She says, "Money has been infected with a lot of scary symbolism, such as that it's evil, gauche, low-class, and common.

"If you remove your ego from the process of making money, you can cure yourself of these unhealthy attitudes. When I worked for other firms, I had the chance to rehearse the role of asking for money without anxiety because it was for the company, not for me. Slowly, I transferred this process to myself.

"It's important to recognize that when you quote a price, the customer is supposed to be more shocked than you are. Remember, most people are uncomfortable talking about money, and if you can discuss money candidly you will have a tremendous advantage. You'll come to recognize money as a tool, neither good nor evil. Once you have the ability to appraise the value of your work, you'll know it isn't gauche to have the self-esteem to ask for every cent your services are worth."

Sumie is right. If you can strip away the myths, you will be able to think clearly about money and get what you are worth. One way to do this might be to treat your first sale as an important symbol of your worth. Hang on to that dollar. Frame it and put it in a place where it will be a daily reminder of your success.

One entrepreneurial friend not only has her first dollar, she also has the first dollar earned in each of her *dad's* stores from more than fifty years back.

If the only economics you've thought of lately is home economics, welcome to the other side of the consumer-oriented economy where getting paid for your talent, your services, your taste, or the ambience you create is a terrific boost.

Vivien Wilson launched her junior boutique in a new shopping center as part of the center's grand-opening festivities. This was a new venture for her, and she was really scared.

That first sale

"I didn't know if I'd be ready for the opening, if I had bought the kind of merchandise that would sell, if people would like my taste. I didn't know what to charge for the handcraft items. I didn't know if one part-time salesperson and I could handle the crowds—if the crowds came—or if we would sit there all alone in the store for lack of customers. What I *did* know, however, is that I had a lot of money invested in this place and everything was riding on its success.

"After that first weekend, when the store was crowded and the center was a success, I was on a cloud. I knew I was really in business! It was so exciting, in fact, that I took the entire weekend's receipts over to my insurance agent to show her. I hadn't believed in myself or my business enough to buy insurance before I opened, but those initial sales gave me such an expanded feeling of self-worth that now I'm committed. I've bought insurance, hired a full-time salesperson, and ordered more merchandise. I have to pinch myself to believe it!"

That kind of disbelief is common among entrepreneurial women, and the highs don't stop after the first sale, either.

A fashion designer said, "It never ceases to amaze me when I see the clothes I've designed and manufactured hanging on the racks in stores. People really do want my creations. They keep on buying them, and they're so expensive! It's a reaffirmation of everything I've worked for, but it also gives me a funny feeling. It's like my babies have left home and I have to stop myself from gathering them up and bringing them back to the factory where they're loved and protected. I know it sounds strange, but they're part of me. It's terrific when I meet someone wearing one of my designs and she tells me how much she loves it and how great it makes her feel. That's the kind of feedback I love to get. It lets me know my 'baby' will have love and a good home."

Not every manufacturer is that closely tied to her product, but most agree at some level with the above statement. Cleo Baldon, of Baldon Galper Associates, an architectural design firm in Venice, California says:

The Entrepreneurial Woman

"I've been in business for thirty years, and it's still exciting when my creations sell. The biggest thrill of all, though, is when I meet an individual who's bought a piece of my furniture at the retail price. It's a very personal thing—it means she has exchanged her working hours for mine. Manufacturers must buy designs, it's part of their business, but when an individual buys, it means they've selected my pieces from the wide choice of furniture out there."

Sales are a great high—almost like coming into an inheritance or winning the Irish Sweepstakes. Only in this case you may feel like you're part of a conspiracy or even feel guilty when people buy what you're selling, and at the price you're asking. Maybe it is better to give than to receive—but not in business! Think of that commercial that says it's OK to pay a little bit more, because you're worth it. Well isn't the reverse also true? Can't you charge a little more (or a *lot* more) because you're worth it?

Think of it this way, life insurance salesmen say a wife is worth more than $20,000 a year. Street sweepers in San Francisco earn $18,000 a year, plumbers earn $20 to $30 an hour. How much are you worth? If you're in a service business, you must set a price for your time. But even in a product-oriented business, your time is part of the cost of doing business.

Someone once said, "Business is like a bowl of spaghetti—all you have to do is find the first strand."

For many entrepreneurs, the first strand is setting a price for products and services. In a service business, the only thing you have to sell is your time and your talents, so developing the psyche to charge someone what your talent is worth is a big step. Women who create their own products face the same problems, since they're putting a price on their creativity.

Janet Carnay, a potter whose specialty is glazing, learned to set a price on her work based on the experience of fellow artists in her community. Her work has won awards in juried shows and she has a growing reputation in her field. She says: "I'm emerging as an artist. I'm really not in business, since I'm not a production

That first sale

person, but my work brings an economic return. My work is one-of-a-kind, but I recognize my potential as an artist and know that it can grow in value as I continue to develop my skill, ability, and knowledge, and reputation. It happens very naturally."

Very few artists can afford to devote their full time to their art in order to develop their skills and reputation. Libby Platus, a sculptor, was able to supplement her earnings by teaching. Her architectural scale-fiber sculpture and sculptural furniture is sold nationwide, and since she now does her work on commission, she is able to put her full energies into her work. Her reputation has reached the point where she earns a substantial income.

There are formulas to guide you in pricing, but formulas won't help you overcome your feelings about money. According to Pamela Dewey, a California fashion designer, when you're willing to pay other creative people the price they ask for their work, then you'll be able to set a price on your own talent and time. And you'll give yourself a fair price.

If you're an artist selling your crafts, you'll be guided by the market for items like those you're producing. But sometimes intangibles enter into the pricing of creative products. The higher the price, the more people will value your work! The same holds true for certain creative services, such as catering.

One caterer told me: "I pulled an outrageous figure out of the air when a very wealthy person asked what I charged for a dinner party. And do you know what happened? She bought it without blinking an eye, and since that time my business has taken off with the country club set in this town."

There's an old story of how to quote a price for a service. Tell the customer your fee is $5,000. If he doesn't gasp, say, "per month," and if he still doesn't gasp, say, "plus expenses," and if there's still no audible response, say, "plus materials."

At the beginning, though, most entrepreneurs in service businesses set their prices in a casual fashion. One woman said that she put a price on her time and then doubled it, but after a year in the public relations business, she found out that she was

The Entrepreneurial Woman

still coming in low. "Keep in mind that it's easier to lower prices than it is to raise them," she said.

She went on to say that the best way of all for her to do business is to put her clients on a monthly retainer and to charge her hours off against that fee. She found the hardest thing to do was estimate how much time a job would take. In order to be able to ask for a retainer, however, you have to have a certain amount of credibility.

Sales help you build credibility, confidence, and contacts. Remember Loré Caulfield's story from Chapter Seven? Success in selling to Fifth Avenue stores in New York (after the airlines had put her on the wrong flight) was such an exhilarating experience that she felt she could have flown to Dallas without a plane. She had much more confidence at Neiman-Marcus than she would have had without that experience. And the fact that she had sold to the top stores in the country increased her credibility and brought her many contacts with other buyers and the media.

How can you use sales to your advantage and bring in more sales? One place you can toot your horn easily is with your suppliers. After all, they like to know how well their goods are selling in your place and what you're doing to make them sell. Manufacturers don't get that kind of feedback often. The following story was told to me by a sharp designer who was looking for promotion help. It's a good example of how your suppliers can work for you.

"Our firm has done some really fabulous jobs this year, but we can't afford to pay for broad-scale advertising, and we don't know the right people to get our pictures and story in the trade magazines. We decided to tell all our suppliers how great their carpets, tiles, wallpaper, or whatever looked in the jobs we'd done. One carpet supplier was so impressed with our story of some walls we'd carpeted in a savings and loan that he sent a photographer out to get a picture of the job. One thing led to another, and the next thing we heard, he wanted to use the picture in his national advertising. Our firm will get the design

That first sale

credit and free publicity! It really is good business to keep your suppliers informed, although we had never expected such positive results. Now that we know suppliers can work this way, we're actively seeking publicity through their resources. After all, their promotional budgets are much larger than ours."

Your sales can also help you increase contacts by word-of-mouth advertising. When you deliver a quality product or go the extra mile in service, word gets around.

But what if you think your sales are increasing because you're charging so little? How can you tell if you're letting yourself be cheated because of your ignorance? Is there a way to figure out what the going rate is for your services? Certainly there is. You can be your own market research company, and here's how.

Call your competitors and ask their prices. Pose as a customer and you'll be surprised at all the information you'll get over the phone. For instance, say you're setting up a silk-screening operation to paint T-shirts. You have some standard designs and you know what to charge for them, but you don't know what the going rate is for custom designs. Ask! "I'm interested in purchasing some T-shirts for my bowling team and we want a special design created just for us. No, I don't have any ideas, but we all agree we would like it to represent something on the order of the liberated mothers' bowling association. You can think of something, can't you? Oh, good. Well, what would you charge for something like that?"

Easy isn't it? Although a little sneaky, it's done every day in business. You'll know you've made it when competitors start calling you!

If you can't call a competitor to find out about pricing because what you offer is so unique, there are formulas to guide you. You should take into consideration your costs, your overhead, the selling price, and the sales volume. The first thing you'll have to do in setting your price will be to figure out your costs. This will include not only your materials and direct labor, but also your overhead. Overhead includes items such as office or store rental,

The Entrepreneurial Woman

secretarial services, telephone and answering service, business stationery and supplies, postage, automotive expenses, licenses and taxes, printing and copying, accounting and legal fees, subscriptions and dues, marketing costs, and other expenses.

Marketing expense is tricky to calculate correctly, especially if you're in a service business where you may be spending thirty to forty percent of your time building up a clientele by direct marketing. When you're taking prospective clients to lunch the costs add up! That's all part of the cost of doing business.

If you're a consultant, you'll have to figure out a billing rate based on your overhead, your salary requirements, and your direct expenses, to which you add a profit margin. As your reputation and credibility increase, so can your profit margin.

Even in a product-oriented business, you'll need to figure out your overhead to establish your breakeven point. For example, Tillie Johnson used this formula in pricing her dolls.

"I knew the price of fabric, stuffing, yarn, and other materials necessary to complete each doll. To this we added the price of reproducing the photo on the face, the cost of direct labor, and packaging expenses. Then we took that figure and doubled it to arrive at our retail price. The markup of 100 percent was to cover our overheads—the costs of our office rental, payroll, licenses and taxes, office supplies, automotive expenses, advertising, telephone, and other incidental expenses—and profit. In a mail-order business such as ours, the overhead is minimal, so we built in quite a comfortable profit margin. The customer paid for the product and the shipping when the order was placed, so we never had a cash-flow problem."

Since she knew no other business quite like hers, Tillie had to arrive at her own pricing formula. Most other product-oriented businesses will have the competition and the market to guide them when they set up their selling prices.

In some businesses, other factors need to be considered. Remember, you always have to be prepared for that unpleasant surprise. Consider the case of this importer and her hidden costs.

That first sale

"In this business it's impossible to figure out the costs of duty and shipping. You never know how the Indonesians or the Italians are going to pack the things you order. If it's clothing and they hang them up in the boxes and ship them air freight, you'll end up paying for the space in the bottom of the box. I thought that if I quadrupled the price of my direct, known costs, I'd be all right, but that wasn't the way it worked out. There's no way to learn except by experience. I finally decided to sell my merchandise to the buyers at FOB the factory. That's the wholesale price plus shipping, duty, and delivery. But it took me a few months before I realized that was the only way to proceed. In the beginning I had to absorb the hidden costs, and that was no way to earn a profit!"

Another importer discussed the cost of "doing business" in many countries of the world. What she was talking about was bribery! It's not just the giant industrialists who have to "do business that way." According to her, it's a fact of life in many countries that if you want to get your goods shipped, you'll have to pay the price.

Other manufacturers and sales representatives have told me of the necessity for building in a five percent "advertising allowance" to the unit price of their product. Sometimes this five percent goes to pay for advertising, but sometimes it goes into the buyer's pocket.

Generally, retailers mark up their goods 100 percent. That is supposed to guarantee a profit by allowing fifty percent to cover their overhead expenses. But selling price alone can be misleading. Often, if you offer items at less than a 100 percent markup, volume makes up for the difference. Look at Rita's story, for example.

"I decided I was really going to make a killing on some warm-up suits in my sporting goods shop. I bought twelve dozen designer outfits at $50 per unit. I knew they were selling in all the department stores for about $100, so I decided to sell them for $79.95. It was Christmas and I ran a small ad in the local paper.

The Entrepreneurial Woman

You'd have thought I was giving something away. They sold out in two weeks. I never turned over merchandise that fast. In those two weeks I made a profit of over $4,000 on the warm-up suits alone! Since my shop is small I had to keep a lot of the merchandise in my home, but as the suits sold, I brought more to the shop. It worked so well I'm doing the same thing this year."

The ingredients in profit making must include: costs, selling price, and sales volume. No single pricing formula will work for every situation. As with Rita, an entrepreneurial woman needs to know her market, what it will bear, and its seasonal variations.

There are two basic rules of pricing, according to the SBA, and these are important for businesswomen to keep in mind. The first is to recognize that it is the market, not your costs, that determines the price at which your products will sell. The second is to be aware of your bottom-line price, or the lowest price at which you can sell your product and still make a profit. Trust your intuition, though. In some cases, you may be able to add thirty percent to the bottom-line price of a product and it will still sell well. People often believe "anything expensive must be good."

Once you've established that you have certain goods or services people want and are willing to pay for, what do you do about it?

Let people know about it. One entrepreneur sends out quarterly newsletters in which she shares the success stories of her clients. (Her business is conducting career-planning and assertiveness-training seminars.) This builds her word-of-mouth advertising and brings in a steady source of new business.

If a newsletter doesn't seem right for your particular business, consider notifying the trade publications or local media of your success. If you run a public relations agency and you land a big new account, you, of all people, should know how to make that newsworthy!

Develop a mailing list of your customers and use it. When your business adds a new product or service, tell your customers and prospective customers about it. Keep your name in the public

That first sale

eye. Remember, in business, too, it's "out of sight, out of mind."

Pay attention to the outside world and pay attention to trends. Susie Bloom did this, and it paid off with a new service to her boutique. Susie noticed that many of her customers were working women who never had time to shop. Some of them came in only twice a year, complaining about what a chore it was to outfit themselves. That did it for Susie! She sent out announcements introducing a unique new service called One-Stop Shopping, which offers her customers the services of a fashion coordinator. Two evenings a week, her store is open by appointment to only five customers. She has a special salesperson to coordinate outfits for her customers and carries a complete line of accessories: handbags, belts, scarves, jewelry—everything except shoes. Now she's thinking of adding a shoe line too. Her new service has increased business and built loyalty among her customers. Susie found that women are willing to pay more for extra service and quality. The clothes she now carries are of a higher quality because of the influence of her new fashion coordinator and this increases Susie's profit margin, since the markup is greater on designer apparel than on mass-produced, ready-to-wear merchandise.

What new service or product can you add to your business? The experts will tell you to be single-minded in purpose, but I'm sure they would agree that it's all right to go from a product to a line. If you're producing and marketing a game successfully, why not take the next step and offer your customers a second product, and eventually a line? Think of how you can build your sales successes into even broader sales.

Julie Lopp Karno wanted to take advantage of the foot traffic from her Grandma's Fudge shops. Since most of her customers were one-time vacation spenders, she knew gift items would be a good source of extra income. She decided to sell copper pots and Early American miniatures. They added to the decor and fit in with the image she had created in her shops. She was able to use all the available space, and the gift items increased her profits

The Entrepreneurial Woman

without actually adding substantially to her costs.

If you're manufacturing a unique item or offering a unique service, have you thought about making personal appearances as part of your marketing effort? Polly Bergen built a large cosmetics business by making personal appearances in department stores. You don't have to be a movie star to build your business that way—Jean Nidetch of Weight Watchers did the same thing.

Another way to keep your name in the public eye is through paid advertising. Anyone who's in business knows you have to spend money to make money. Tillie Johnson was amazed at the cost of her ad in the Sunday supplement magazine of her hometown newspaper. She had to pay for the advertising layout as well as the cost of placing the ad, but it was money well-spent. Her sales volume increased tremendously because of that ad, and the additional sales paid for it many times over.

Now that your confidence is increasing, be creative. People want what you're selling. Look for other ways to promote your business.

If you have an apparel shop, you might try putting on a fashion show to highlight your clothes for the local women's club. Or, if you have a hobby supply shop, consider offering classes at a minimal fee to potential customers. They'll buy their materials from you and you'll have a whole new group of hobbyists as a source of business.

The entrepreneurial women mentioned here had to draw upon their creativity to broaden their market. You'll have to draw upon yours too. It's important to be knowledgeable about your industry and to keep in touch with new trends. What's happening in the rest of the world *does* affect your business, and not only in broadening your market. Sometimes these trends will affect whether or not you'll be able to hold onto your present market.

In the next chapter you'll read the story of one entrepreneurial woman who failed to watch the trends. She let her enthusiasm get out of hand. Chapter Eleven—on bankruptcy—contains more than one good lesson for you.

$$$$$$$$ 11 $$$$$$$$
Bankruptcy can be beautiful

We can do anything we want if we stick to it long enough.
—Helen Keller

Webster's dictionary defines bankruptcy as failure, reduction to a state of complete impoverishment, and ruin. The law says you are bankrupt when you owe more than you own and can't pay your debts. People who have gone bankrupt agree with all of the above but find Webster's definition lacking in force. They add words like defeat, despair, doom, and even degradation.

A determined entrepreneur, however, doesn't view bankruptcy as death but rather as a temporary setback. The true entrepreneur never says die, even though she may contemplate suicide at first.

In this chapter we'll look at some stories of financial reverses. Then you can decide if bankruptcy can be beautiful.

Carole Sumner-Appel had been designing residential and commercial interiors in Los Angeles for six years when an oportunity came along that was too good to pass up. She had eight employees at the time and was doing well, but she saw this opportunity as a chance to make an enormous amount of money. An acquaintance who was promoting a condominium development at Mammoth Mountain, a ski resort in California, suggested that she decorate the model unit. In fact, why not furnish all forty apartments? He said he had sold one hundred units the year before, and in his experience they sold faster if they were prefurnished. He promised to buy the first twenty units and act as

The Entrepreneurial Woman

her sales agent to move the others. It seemed like a sure-fire thing for both of them. He would be able to sell the condominiums fast, and she would be able to maximize her profits.

She would have to buy the furnishings up front, but Carole felt she could make a killing, so she took the risk. To pull it off she needed a $25,000 loan. She went to the bank with her proposal, and they bought it. All she had to do was sign her name. Now she was a packager and on her way to making big money!

She got right to work designing the layouts, ordering the furniture, and arranging to ship the materials for the first twenty units. She was already counting her money. She arrived in Mammoth with a caravan of trucks filled with furniture, only to be greeted by a snowstorm. The drivers couldn't get anyone to unload the merchandise and they threatened to turn around and take the goods back to Los Angeles. Carole was frantic, but she wasn't going to let the situation defeat her. She thought, "It's snowing—a blizzard—the lifts must be closed—skiers, instructors, strong young men must be sitting around doing nothing." So she went to the local radio station and appealed to anyone wanting work to come and help. They came—fifteen strong young men!

Once Carole had solved that problem, she thought she was home free. All she had to do was sit back and wait for the customers and the money to start coming in. It was snowing, and in Mammoth snow is money. But oil is also money, and just when Carole was mentally spending the dollars, the oil crisis hit. No one could get to Mammoth to buy her beautifully designed units. It was a disaster.

Not one of the packages sold, and she was in serious trouble. Everybody in the ski area was going bankrupt around her. Nobody could pay any bills. She never got paid for her designs. And because she didn't get paid for her designs, she couldn't pay the supplier. It was that simple. She had extended herself to about $90,000 and didn't have any money! "I had 125 creditors," she said, "and no money. It sank in—I was really in trouble!

Bankruptcy can be beautiful

"I remember the meeting in my office when all my advisers—my dad, my attorney, and a business consultant—told me to forget it. They said I had no right to be in business. They told me that with all the money I owed and with the number of creditors I had, there was no way to turn it around. I was beating my head against a stone wall, they said, and I'd have an emotional breakdown if I persisted. They told me to declare bankruptcy. But a wonderful friend convinced me not to give up. He knew my potential and told me I had too much going for me to let it all go, so with his help and my attorney's this is what we did.

"I was honest and straight with all my creditors. I told them the truth, that's all. And let me tell you, honesty and truth will work for you every time. Since I had been in business six and a half years and had dealt with most of these suppliers, they all knew who I was. I had always paid my bills on time and had been a good customer. So I explained the situation to them. I said I enjoyed our business association and wanted to continue it, but that I couldn't pay my bills right now. If I could in the future, I would, and if I couldn't, I wouldn't. I was very frightened, but because I was straight with them, they all went along. Nobody pushed me into bankruptcy—and they certainly could have. After that it was COD with all these suppliers, but eventually our business association got back on a solid footing. You know, I'm still doing business with all of them, and most of them have even forgiven the debt. They know it's a fact of business—everybody runs into trouble now and then.

"This all happened about four years ago, and since that time, my business has really turned around. I'd take the risk again. I learned that failure can be a tremendous success experience if you'll learn from it. I know that no matter how smart anyone is, sooner or later you make a bad decision. And that's what happened to me."

Carole's financial reverses energized her to keep going, and she pulled it off. But bankruptcy isn't that beautiful for everyone. Take Amanda Howard's story for example.

The Entrepreneurial Woman

Amanda came to New York at the age of twenty with eighty dollars in her pocket. She had been supporting herself for the previous five years by sewing and designing clothes, starting at the age of fifteen in an Albany bridal shop, and eventually had opened her own clothing business in Toronto. She had been on her own since she was a teenager, and her dream was to get a job in the textile industry designing fabrics.

She began sewing for her friends in New York, and soon two women with a Third Avenue boutique discovered her and hired her as their designer. They gave her bolts of fabric and told her to do what she wanted. They made a lot of money, and so did she. But Amanda needed to recharge herself after working hard for several months, so she took off for Europe to study and learn more about art, history, fashion, and design.

While she was in Europe, the two women split up their partnership. On her return, one of them called Amanda and offered her a partnership. She went into business with her ex-boss, but it soon became apparent that it wasn't going to work out. Amanda saw she was involved in some kind of psychological warfare with her partner. One day she came into the shop and everything was gone: the inventory, the partner, the money. The only things left were the debts. And Amanda was left holding the bag!

It almost destroyed Amanda. For months, she couldn't sew. Every time she got near her sewing machine, she became physically ill. It was a time of great emotional and physical turmoil. Fortunately, she found a job with a design firm. The owner and his wife recognized her potential as an artist and encouraged her. Today Amanda is back in the fashion business, having recovered from the devastation of bankruptcy.

She says, "It takes more guts to try and fail than not to try at all. If you can learn to believe in yourself, you merely have to find the right direction. It's the holes in the road that get you off the track. You'll have accidents because you can't always see the holes."

Bankruptcy can be beautiful

Norma Saken, whom we met in Chapter Nine, found her catering business took more time than she wanted it to. She was earning a great deal of money, but had no time to enjoy it. For a divorcee with two young children, her life left a lot to be desired. She had no time for a social life, no time with her children, and no energy left at the end of the day. She had weird working hours, and on top of it all, there was no involvement in the glamour and fun of the elegant parties she catered. She and her partner decided to do something else.

"My partner and I made a lot of money in our catering business. We knew that the government would get most of it in taxes if we didn't do something with it soon. So we decided to open a cheesecake bakery. I had a terrific recipe from my grandmother, and we took it around to all the finest restaurants in town to see if they would buy it. They said they would, and that was the extent of our market research.

"We bought the newest and finest equipment we could find, and we were in business again. We continued to use our name, Saycheese, because it had worked so well for us before. We were in business for three months when I realized we didn't really know anything about business. We had just been lucky before.

"This time we couldn't charge outrageous prices, and nobody cared that we were young, personable, and attractive. The only thing they cared about was our cheesecake. It had no preservatives, and it cost too much to make. There were only so many restaurants that could afford to buy a ten-dollar cheesecake. We thought everyone would beat a path to our door because we had the greatest cheesecake, but we were wrong. We had no working capital, and just before Christmas we went bankrupt.

"I didn't have a cent, so I took a job demonstrating cookware in a department store. Misfortune has a way of getting to me. On top of everything else, my appendix burst, I got peritonitis, and I had to go into the county hospital—on welfare! That was the bottom. There wasn't any place to go but up from there. But, I'm a

The Entrepreneurial Woman

survivor—I don't come from Russian peasant stock for nothing!"

So what's happened to all our bankrupt entrepreneurs?

Carole, Amanda, and Norma are all back on the road to financial independence, freedom, and success. In fact, every one of them agrees that in order to understand what success was all about, they had to experience the pain of failure.

Carole's business is booming. In fact, that wonderful friend who convinced her to stay in business has joined the firm and is now her husband. The direction of her business has changed, and she's moved from residential and office interiors to very large, detailed jobs. Her firm, Sumner and Associates, is now called Interior Architects. One look at their drawings and designs and you'd understand why. A skating rink on which they've worked for nine months required detailed specifications for the entire interior. It is actually a guide for the architect to plan a building around. The firm is involved in the conceptual process, the design, specifications to implement the design, and the supervision of the project. Working on this scale is certainly a departure from the days of furnishing model homes.

Amanda, too, has had a wonderful success as a designer in the eight years since her bankruptcy experience. Her firm specializes in women's leisure wear. She produces two lines a year—summer and winter—and she's been featured in all the leading fashion magazines. Her clothes are sold nationally at the finest department stores.

Amanda's renewed energy, drive, and accomplishments have given her much pleasure. She has what it takes for entrepreneurial success and she's proved it by her determination to succeed.

And what about Norma? What's happened to her since the burst appendix? Well, Norma is still alive and kicking, only not as frantically this time around. She is now a space representative for a national travel magazine. Being a space rep is also an entrepreneurial venture—one in which Norma must draw upon the same skills she used so well in her catering venture.

Bankruptcy can be beautiful

"After my appendix burst," Norma recalls, "I was flat broke. There I was, the mother of two young children, and sick. My Dad said, 'This is it! You've got six months to learn a trade. After that you're on your own.' Since my cousin was a manicurist, my Dad thought it would be a good field for me, and he packed me off to manicuring school. What a mistake! When I graduated, I got a job at Saks and was there only one day when I realized I would never last filing the nails of the women with whom I used to go shopping. I was desperate, and I still had to pay the rent at the end of the week. I needed a job. What to do? This time, I knew it was up to me.

"I saw an ad for a girl friday. I couldn't type and had never been a girl friday, but I guess I was so pathetic that the woman, who has since become my mentor, hired me. She, too, had been a single mother supporting a family, so she knew exactly what I was going through. Fortunately for me, she understood the juggling act I'd been doing.

"My boss sold magazine advertising space to various advertising managers in the territory, and I was there about nine months when I realized I could do that. So I told her about my ambitions and she said, go to it! I didn't waste time learning how, I just went out and did it. Now I know what I'm doing. It took me six months to land a really big account, but I did. Now I get the travel ads from the Mexican government, the Mexican hotel industry, and the Mexican airlines. I love what I do. I finally figured out that I don't belong in a corporation—I'm too independent for that and I can't play the political games necessary to survive in the corporate environment.

"The experiences I've had in the past few years have given me a stronger sense of my own self-worth. I'm no longer living hand-to-mouth, and it's a great feeling to know I have a cash flow again. I know I'm OK because the commissions keep coming in!"

Pretty heady stuff, these bankruptcy stories. But the important lesson to learn from these stories is that it wasn't the end. It wasn't utter ruin. Failure is never fun. It does hurt. But it can help

The Entrepreneurial Woman

you turn your life around if you learn from it. Sometimes failure can bring you a peculiar kind of freedom. You're free to do or not to do. You can relax. The worst has already happened. By not having to try so hard, you're suddenly free to see new possibilities. Your failure can contribute to your personal growth.

One entrepreneurial woman who decided to close her business after two grueling years said, "I don't see what I did in terms of failure or mistakes. I know I'll take a lot of flak from 'friends' who advised me against going into business, but I didn't lose money and I didn't fail. I made a decision, that's all. At least now I know I'm comfortable enough with myself to *make* a decision!"

That statement says a great deal, and gets right to the heart of the issue. Everything begins and ends with inner confidence and intuitive feelings. Remember the saying, "If it is to be, it's up to me." Well, the only way you'll ever make your small business into a bigger business is to learn how to juggle money, and that involves risks. But the main ingredient will always be you. You will be the one to sell the idea to your banker, your accountant, and your attorney. If you believe in yourself and your talent, and if you can ask people for help and advice, who knows? You might even break the bank!

$$$$$$$$ 12 $$$$$$$$
Achievement and its rewards

Too much of a good thing can be wonderful.
—Mae West

What if you do break the bank? What if your hard work and determination pay off and you really do strike it rich? Can you handle achievement and success? This is not a flip question; many people have somewhat schizophrenic reactions to success. Are you ready to accept the rewards of having your own business? Do you know the rewards?

In this final chapter, you'll read about the rewards of entrepreneurial achievement. Rewards like new freedom, fame, fortune, and the realization of your dreams. You'll gain new insights into the man-woman relationships, and the pleasures of belonging to the "new woman's" network. These rewards and achievements go beyond the kind you read about in "How to Start Your Own Business" handbooks.

Consider Anna. Anna is an eccentric actress who loves being, as she puts it, "crazy." Now, for most of us, that doesn't seem like the greatest qualification for going into business, but it's perfect for Anna. She and her friend Phyllis, a gourmet cook, decided on a lark to open a small restaurant. They called the place "Anna's Bananas," and specialized in banana dishes. It was located in a small eastern vacation town and was a perfect setup for the two of them. Phyllis was married with three children and was feeling trapped in her role as wife and mother. She wanted to see if she could do something on her own. This gave her a chance to get out of her kitchen for a while and put her

The Entrepreneurial Woman

talents to work in a professional capacity. Anna was able to be as eccentric as she ever wanted to be. Best of all, she was eccentric in the name of fun and profit.

Anna dressed as Chiquita Banana and played promoter, hostess, and actress at the same time. She even got some props from a theatrical house in New York to augment the decor. Phyllis was happy cooking in her kitchen and keeping the books. Their speciality was banana bread and frozen banana delight. During the warm summer months they sold chocolate-covered frozen bananas by the hundreds. Anna soon learned her real skill was in public relations; she excelled in promoting the business to every tourist and vacationer in the area. She even made some contacts for the future, since she knew the venture was seasonal and the partnership would probably be temporary.

Here's what Anna gained from her two summers as a banana tycoon. "The business gave me the chance to find out who I was and to learn that I could support myself and have fun at the same time. It brought me freedom and confidence. I knew I would never have to work for anyone again. I could depend on myself and my talents to see me through. Now I do freelance public relations. I work when and where I choose. My fee is substantial, and fortunately I'm able to support myself very well. I work with clients on my own terms, and because I'm successful, I guess they forgive my eccentricity."

I asked Anna what had happened to her former partner. She said, "Phyllis, too, learned a great deal about herself the summer we worked together. Before we started she was having a difficult time integrating her search for independence with marriage and motherhood, which she valued. Those two summers away from her family were a growing period for her. Once she discovered she could be financially independent and make decisions on her own, it wasn't so difficult going back to her family. She's come to a more positive self-realization. Now, I think she's in France going to the Cordon Bleu cooking school. She's doing what she wants to, and that's just great."

Achievement and its rewards

When I asked her how she made out in the business, Anna responded, "We didn't lose money, but we didn't make a lot either. We hadn't really expected to. We supported ourselves, and I earned enough to tide me over until I found a job back in New York. But at that stage in my life it seemed like big business!"

Another pair of women who started an equally eccentric venture five years ago watched theirs grow into a genuine big business. Toby Brown and Lila Greene are Los Angeles housewives and co-founders of Renta Yenta International, a business noted for ingenuity and outlandish creativity. They provide everything from live elephants to belly dancers and marching bands for parties, special events, and individual surprises—and have a great time doing it.

"We were two housewives looking for a way to get out of the house, to pay housekeepers to watch our children. But we had no skills and no 'front-office appeal' [an expression used in the employment business referring to nubile young women]. We began with a twelve-dollar ad in *Variety*, stating, 'ANYTHING YOU CAN'T DO WE CAN—RENTA YENTA.' [*Yenta* is a Yiddish term for a woman who knows everything about everybody and everything—a busybody.]

"Our business has grown into an operation with licensees in twenty-five cities in the United States and one in Montreal. We have our own catering business, and we serve many celebrities. But one of our biggest thrills was when we sold our story to Warner Brothers for a situation comedy."

So, no matter how far out your idea seems to others—or to you—take yourself seriously. Let them laugh at you, and you too may end up as the inspiration for a movie. Or you might end up laughing with them—all the way to the bank.

Toby and Lila are pleased that their creativity contributes to the success of parties they plan for their clients. But there are many more rewards for entrepreneurial women.

For instance, Loré Caulfield, of Loré Lingerie, says "It's so gratifying to see the people I employ in my business happy and

The Entrepreneurial Woman

productive. Three of my employees are Vietnamese refugees, two are from Korea, one is American, one is a recent Russian Jewish emigré, and two are young black men. It's like one big, happy family. I had a special sense of gratification from watching two of my seamstresses become friends. They don't speak the same language, but every day they have lunch together, and after work walk out arm-in-arm to the bus. To think that one of them came here from the poverty and misery of Vietnam only a few years ago. It is so rewarding now to see her happy. I never expected my business to deliver rewards like this."

Loré went on to say, "Business, for me, is not a cold, impersonal thing. It's a monument to personal endeavor, and now is the time for women to get a piece of the monument."

Loré has had her share of material rewards as well. She has a beautiful New York City penthouse apartment that also doubles as a showroom. She does not object to the buying trip to Hong Kong that her business affords her, nor to the annuity it provides. It has also given her the freedom to go back to her first love—producing, writing, and directing movies. Actually, her business started because her husband thought she should put together a cottage industry to help support her creative movie ventures. Some cottage industry!

Consider the rewards Jackie Cappelli has found. Her dream was to one day own a racehorse. Well, her Mother-and-Daughter boutique gave her the opportunity to realize that dream, and her horse has even won its first race!

Sally Stanford, the San Francisco former-madam-turned-restauranteur, found that her entrepreneurial tenacity served her well in being elected mayor of Sausalito, California. In spite of the fact that she had lost six previous elections for the city council, her determination drove her to run one more time. That time she won. People without entrepreneurial spirit would have given up.

Working hard for future freedom is the goal of many entrepreneurial women. Elaine Wegener and Noreen St. Pierre are willing to work sixteen hours a day, seven days a week to earn

Achievement and its rewards

enough to pursue future creative ventures. Noreen looks forward to a career in music while Elaine wants more time for writing.

An important issue among entrepreneurial women, as we discussed earlier, is the new kind of relationship some are finding with men.

A boutique owner talked about an unexpected dividend. "I used to resent my husband not coming home for dinner. Now, it's a liberating experience. My kids and I eat out a lot. MacDonald's hamburgers are gourmet fare for them, and I don't have to eat—it's an easy way to diet. 'What's for dinner?' used to be my biggest concern—it was the main event of my day. Now that I have my own business, I care more about other things. My self-confidence is growing—I no longer look for validation by my performance at the dinner hour."

See what can happen to a woman who starts thinking about money instead of food? She went on to say, "Now, I've got an unlimited opportunity for making money. And the added benefit is that my husband doesn't have to feel guilty anymore about not coming home for dinner."

Some women use men in support roles, helping them to get their businesses off the ground. Listen to what Carole Sumner-Appel's husband, Sheldon, says.

"All my life I was a star. I was out there in front in my electronics business and in the music business. But now Carole's the star, and I take a back seat. I love it. It's the best thing that's ever happened to me. Carole is sensational, and it's such a great feeling seeing her do something creative. It's hard for a lot of men. They have a macho complex with women, but let me tell you my role. It's management and guidance. I'm a calming influence on Carole. She can do anything. Sometimes she has eight projects going at once. She's so creative she doesn't always think of the financial aspects of her creativity. I help her by writing contracts and taking the money problems off her mind. Now I'm the one they have to talk to about money, and that frees Carole to engage in all types of creative work.

The Entrepreneurial Woman

"We work well together. Carole and I understand each other's limits and strengths. She's a fantastic salesperson—she has the spark. And I've learned to stay out of the creative side of the business. We have a mutual respect for each other's ability. I have great respect for women. Women are stronger than men. If you put a woman and a man together in business, and that woman has the tenacity, the sky's the limit. The problem, as I see it, is that women are fighting men. They should work together with men, use their knowledge, hire some men, whatever it takes. We can use our knowledge of money in helping businesswomen."

We can find supportive men. True men of quality are not frightened by equality. But all husband-wife business involvements are not that easy. It depends on the man's ego. Some husbands find it hard to believe that "the little woman" who washed his socks could possibly know anything about running a business. A husband may find it difficult to keep quiet when he comes into his wife's establishment and she's not running it according to his business school logic. Your husband may have something of value to offer, but if his overall message is negative, try to keep him as far away from your business as possible. It's hard enough to believe in yourself without having to put up with a nit-picking husband. He's got to believe in you enough to allow you to make your own mistakes, because that's the only way you'll learn.

Another benefit for entrepreneurial women is the development of women's networks (groups of businesswomen who exchange information and provide support). You may have problems with your friends once you change from your old image of teacher, secretary, PTA official, or housewife into an entrepreneurial woman who never has time for old friends. Well, a woman's network can provide new friends, ones who understand what it is you're up against in the world of business. Since the Rotary Club is still deciding whether women can join, and the Kiwanis haven't even approached the subject, women across the

Achievement and its rewards

country have stopped trying to join the old boys' network and are forming their own.

Groups like the National Association of Women Business Owners, with headquarters in Washington, D.C., or Professional Women's Alliance and Women Entrepreneurs in San Francisco, or Women in Business in Los Angeles have been formed expressly for the purpose of offering support and information, both economic and emotional, to businesswomen.

An importer in Los Angeles needed to move some office furniture. She consulted her handy *Women in Business Directory* and found a female-operated moving company to do the job. Women storeowners are finding women attorneys, women office managers are finding female-owned suppliers, and so on. When we give business to one another, we're supporting the development of a women's economic network. You can form your own group if one doesn't exist in your town. Women in Business has found that a fifty-fifty mix of entrepreneurial and corporate women works best. That way, entrepreneurs learn management and financial tricks from their corporate sisters, and corporate women have a source for all the goods and services they need.

Women can teach other women the rules of the game of business. One entrepreneur in insurance said: "I've been in business for twenty years, with my own brokerage firm. These past few years have been the most exciting for me because I'm giving women financial advice and helping them set up businesses and advising them on protection. It's a whole new era for women."

A whole new era indeed! We're gaining power, but the difficulties of dealing with some male establishment bankers, attorneys, accountants, and insurance experts can't be overlooked. One nice thing about women's networks is that they help steer women to the right financial people—men or women—who can deal fairly with a businesswoman. To some extent, many married entrepreneurs still involve their husbands in legal and financial matters because it's the most expedient thing to do.

The Entrepreneurial Woman

Most say, however, that if they could get through a financial situation without having their husband there to back them up, they would. They object to the necessity of a husband giving the factory tour, talking to the lender, giving the place a general aura of "respectability." If a man is involved in the business, some of the old-fashioned men think it's a much safer venture. That's why it's so important to be part of the new woman's network. A woman can lend you money, and you won't have to showcase a man.

Many men and women aren't prepared for the new messages of achievement being sent out to women. They laugh when they see a female skydiver or airline pilot advertising a feminine product on TV. They think it's far-fetched for a woman jockey to sell products. Slogans such as "There's really nothing you can't do" and "Because you're doing more, you want more" are giving women the message that it's all right to achieve. Madison Avenue merely reflects pronounced trends and mirrors societal changes, it doesn't make them.

Los Angeles entrepreneurs echo the achievement messages of Madison Avenue. They stand very tall and say things like these:

Karen Sandler, interior plant landscaper—"I'm making more money than I ever made before, and it feels good. I like being my own boss and setting my own time schedule. I like the tax benefits and I like belonging to professional organizations. And I love the freedom!"

Sanda Alcalay, owner of French Conversational Seminars and Aubergine and Associates, Catered Affairs—"I get so much pleasure out of taking care of myself and from my clients' feedback. I have the freedom to make my own decisions and set my own goals. I can explore my creativity. The only limits I have are my own and it feels very good. When I started my second business, I would whisper to people about it. Now I look straight at them, smile, and say, 'I own two businesses!' "

Nancy Malone, independent film producer—"As an actor, I complained about the poor roles available for women. Now I'm in a position to do something about it."

Achievement and its rewards

Sara Rosenberg, owner of Wilshire Secretarial Service—"It's such a good feeling helping clients prepare their resumes. It's the first time many have seen their achievements put down in writing. It's almost like a rebirth for them. It raises their self-esteem and allows them to go out and make career changes. I love being part of that process."

Cleo Baldon, partner, Galper Baldon Associates, architectural design—"Designing the ultimate in underwater seating and seeing the development of the Hydro Spa Company as a result of my work was a tremendous high. Seeing a building I designed in the *Guide to Contemporary Architecture* was another rewarding experience. Understanding the mechanics of the craft, and thereby gaining the respect of the craftsmen who manufacture my furniture designs is also very rewarding."

Betty Vokes, owner of Betty Vokes and Associates, real estate—"Negotiating and closing a sale is a great high, especially when my clients really love the house and I've helped them to figure out the financial aspects."

And this statement from a thirteen-year-old Indiana entrepreneur (on the occasion of buying a house with her earnings from her paper route and Christmas card sales)—"I bought this house as an investment. I plan to rent it out, and build a fund to buy another house in two years."

Even the younger generation is finding out about the rewards of entrepreneurship!

Now that you've read about all the rewards, and the wonderful feelings achievement and success can bring, how do you *really* feel about success?

Do you think it's strange to be asked how you feel about success and achievement at this late stage? Especially since the rest of this book has been waving the flags of achievement at you and saying, "You can do it!" Well, it's not so strange, and it's an important issue because a lot of men and women in this country still haven't totally accepted nondomestic achievement by women. Didn't you grow up with statements like Samuel Johnson's "A

The Entrepreneurial Woman

man is in general better pleased when he has a good dinner upon his table than when his wife talks Greek"?

A Los Angeles entrepreneur says this about her achievement and fears.

"I have a fear of success because the pressure would be greater. If I succeed, I'd have to live up to my image. Just before I reach the height, the apex of achievement, I become bored with a project because I know I can do it. Then what other challenges are left? For me, the fun is the anticipation and the challenge of getting the job. Seeing it through doesn't interest me." Is her assesssment true, or is it just another way of avoiding success?

What she said reminded me of my feelings as a twelve-year-old when I was cast as Jo in *Little Women*. It was thrilling being chosen for the part—it meant I was the best. But if I took it, and did well, would my friends be jealous? Would they still like me? Would I be as good in the play as Amy (played by my best friend) or Beth (another friend)? What if I was better? Fear of success and fear of failure created an internal conflict. I quit drama class rather than resolve it.

But my motivation to achieve was still strong, and in my adult years I became more comfortable with competition and achievement. The old voices still return every now and then, and the fears are still there, but I ignore them and move on.

Even though the media are highlighting women's achievements in sports and business, the psychological barriers remain. There hasn't been a total transference from Chris Evert's and Janet Guthrie's sports achievements to the psyches of achieving women. Too many entrepreneurial women call themselves "overachievers." Do we still have to think of ourselves as "overachievers" when we achieve success? Does that imply that achieving women still need to be Wonder Women or Supermoms to be successful?

Matina Horner, president of Radcliffe College, did a study in the early 1970s on women and their achievement motives. She found that bright college women actually equated intellectual

Achievement and its rewards

achievement with a loss of femininity. She said: "A bright woman is caught in a double bind. In achievement-oriented situations she worries not only about failure, but also about success." She called this motivation to avoid achievement "fear of success."

In the motivational seminars and in the individual counseling sessions I've had with businesswomen, this problem constantly surfaces. It's not usually labeled "fear of success," but I believe it is still the underlying issue. I hear questions such as "How can I give my soul to the company and still raise a family?" or "Is there such a thing as a happily married entrepreneurial woman?" I also hear such comments as "I don't want to get married or have children because it can't work for achievement-oriented women" and "There are few men who can accept a successful woman." It seems that no matter how high the consciousness has been raised, women still want warm, loving relationships. And many fear that their business success will stand in the way.

Are you still fighting within yourself? Are your desires to achieve and your fear of success immobilizing you and keeping you from reaching your goals? This internal fight can keep you paralyzed forever. Why not make friends with yourself? Give up the fight, resolve the conflict, and get on with it!

Suggested Reading

Personal Development

Beecher, Willard and Marguerite. *Beyond Success and Failure: Ways to Self-Reliance and Maturity*. New York: The Julian Press, Inc., 1966.

Bliss, Edwin C. *Getting Things Done: The ABC's of Time Management*. New York: Charles Scribner's Sons, 1976.

Bloom, Lynn A.; Coburn, Karen Levin; and Pearlman, Jean Crystal. *The New Assertive Woman*. New York: Delacorte Press, 1975.

Bolles, Richard Nelson. *What Color is Your Parachute?* Berkley: Ten Speed Press, 1972. A manual for job hunters and career changers.

Dible, Donald M. *Up Your Own Organization*. Berkley: Entrepreneur Press, 1974, distributed by Hawthorne Books, New York.

Klimley, April. *Borrowing Basics for Women*. New York: First National City Bank, 1978. Write for free copy to: Public Affairs Division, 399 Park Avenue, New York, N.Y. 10002.

Ruddick, Sara, and Daniels, Pamela. *Working It Out*. New York: Pantheon Books, 1977.

Satir, Virginia. *Peoplemaking*. Palo Alto: Science and Behavior Books, Inc., 1972.

Selye, Hans. *The Stress of Life*. New York: McGraw-Hill, 1976.

Starting and Running a Business

Bank of America, "How to Prepare a Personal Financial Statement." *Consumer Information Report 5 (1976)*.

Chipps, Genie, and Jessup, Calaudia. *The Woman's Guide to Starting a Business*. New York: Holt, Rinehart & Winston, 1976.

Enterprising Women: A Business Monthly. New York: Artemis Enterprises, Inc. This publication is an excellent source of information for the small-business owner. First-hand, step-by-step stories of businesses begun by women are included in each issue.

Fiske, H., and Zehring, K. "How to Start Your Own Business." *Ms.*, April 1976, pp. 55–69.

Greene, G. G. *How to Start and Manage Your Own Business.* Los Angeles: (A Mentor Book) New American Library, 1975.

Hammer, Marian Behan. *The Complete Handbook of How to Start and Run a Money-Making Business in Your Home.* New Jersey: Prentice-Hall, 1975.

Hilton, Terri. *Small Business Ideas for Women—And How to Get Started.* New York: Pilot Books, 1975.

Under Money, "The Entrepreneurs." *Time,* March; April; May; June, 1978.

"Business on a Shoestring." *New Woman.* Fort Lauderdale, Florida; New Woman, Inc. A regular column that briefly reports on businesses begun by women.

Park, William, R. and Park, Sue Chapin. *How To Succeed in Your Own Business.* Salt Lake City: Wiley and Sons, Inc., 1978.

Working Woman. New York: W. W. Publications. Contains regular features on business strategy for entrepreneurial women.

The following are published by the Small Business Administration and are available free from any SBA field office or the Washington, D.C. headquarters.

"Business Plan for Small Manufacturers." *Management Aids for Small Manufacturers, No. 218* (1973). This booklet is a guide to developing a business plan for a small manufacturing firm. If this is your business goal, you will probably want to get a copy of it. Pages 3–9 deal with marketing conditions.

"Business Plan for Small Service Firms." *Small Marketers Aid, No. 153* (1973). A booklet designed to help the future owner-manager of a small service firm develop his or her own plan. Pages 4–9 cover marketing issues.

"Business Plan for Retailers." *Small Marketers Aid, No. 150* (1972). A guide to follow in drawing up a business plan for a small retail firm. Pages 3–8 review the marketing section of the plan.

DeBoer, L. M. "Marketing Research Procedures." *Small Business Bibliography, No. 9* (1974). This bibliography lists and briefly describes a number of books, pamphlets, directories, associations, and magazines that are helpful in learning about and conducting marketing research.

Kress, G., and Will, R.T. "Marketing Checklist for Small Retailers." *Small Marketers Aid*, No. 156 (1974). The questions on consumer analyses, pricing, and promotion (pages 2–6) are worth considering. The checklist provides a good review before you go into business.

Medicalf, W. O. "Starting and Managing A Small Business of Your Own." *The Starting and Managing Series*, No. 1 (1973).

The following are published by and are available from Bank of America, Department 3120, P.O. Box 37000, San Francisco, CA 94137. (Send $1 per copy to cover postage and handling.)

"Steps to Starting a Business." *Small Business Reporter X* (November, 1976).

"Marketing New Product Ideas." *Small Business Reporter X*, 5 (1974). This booklet is particularly geared toward independent inventors and product innovators who want to introduce a new product.

"Advertising Small Business." *Small Business Reporter XIII*, 9 (1977). An excellent and comprehensive guide for use in developing and advertising programs. Useful in any type of business.

"Understanding Financial Statements." *Small Business Reporter VII*, 11 (1974). An excellent, easy-to-read guide.

"Cash Flow/Cash Management." *Small Business Reporter XIII*, 9 (1977). How managing a small company's finances is like handling the household budget.

Women's Issues

Chesler, Phyllis, and Goodman, Emily Jane. *Women, Money, and Power*. New York: William Morrow and Company, 1976.

Cox, Sue. *Female Psychology: The Emerging Self*. Palo Alto: Science Research Associates, Inc., 1976.

Janeway, Elizabeth. *Man's World, Woman's Place*. New York: Dell Publishing Co., 1971.

Loring, Rosaline K., and Otto, Herbert. *New Life Options: The Working Woman's Resource Book*. New York: McGraw-Hill, 1976.

Acknowledgements

My first thanks are to those entrepreneurial women who trusted me with their ideas, stories, and problems. Without their cooperation and encouragement this book would not have been possible.

My gratitude also to my children: to my daughter, Marci, who took charge of proofreading, running copies, and giving me needed support; to my son, Gregg, who provided the motivation to leave the house and go to my office to write; and to my youngest daughter, Robin, who survived an absentee mother and learned the independence necessary for future entrepreneurship.

Thanks also to my mother, Mae Yavitt, for encouraging *my* independence, and to my dad, David Yavitt, from whom I learned how to tell a story.

Special thanks to Alice Allen Donald, my agent, who believed in me and the book, and to Sandy Leonard, who spent many long hours chained to her typewriter pounding out the manuscript.

Above all, it is to my husband, George, that I owe my deepest thanks. Without his sharp pencil and his editorial skill, my work would have been infinitely more difficult. His love and encouragement, his male perspective, and his developing skills as a "house husband" saw me through.

Sandra Winston
Palos Verdes Estates,
California

About The Author

SANDRA WINSTON heads her own consulting firm and is a licensed marriage, family and child counselor. She has special expertise in management and employee development for women, and has conducted training programs for several prestigious business corporations. In addition to her private consulting and counseling practice, she has developed the Emerging Woman and Entrepreneurial Woman programs for UCLA Extension Center for the Continuing Education of Women. Ms. Winston is president and cofounder of STEP, Inc., an adult education corporation in which she conducts life-planning and career-development workshops. She is a graduate of Ohio State University and received her M.Ed. from the University of Cincinnati. Sandra Winston lives in Palos Verdes Estates, California, is married and is the mother of three children.